PSYCHOPATHOLOGY OF WORK

PSYCHOANALYTIC IDEAS AND APPLICATIONS SERIES

Recent titles in the Series
(for a full listing, please visit www.karnacbooks.com)

PSYCHOPATHOLOGY OF WORK

Clinical Observations

Edited by

Christophe Dejours

Translated by

Caroline Williamson

KARNAC

First published in English in 2015 by
Karnac Books Ltd
118 Finchley Road, London NW3 5HT

Published in French in 2010 as *Observations cliniques en psychopathologies du travail* in the «Souffrance et théorie» series by Presses Universitaires de France.

British Library Cataloguing in Publication Data

A C.I.P. for this book is available from the British Library

ISBN 978 1 78220 180 9

Edited, designed and produced by The Studio Publishing Services Ltd
www.publishingservicesuk.co.uk
e-mail: studio@publishingservicesuk.co.uk

Printed in Great Britain

www.karnacbooks.com

CONTENTS

ACKNOWLEDGEMENTS

The various observations collected here have already been the subject of publications in a wide range of specialist publications and journals. Some of these are out-of-print and have become practically inaccessible. Some of the more recent ones have been revised. The original publications are as follows:

Chapter One—Dejours, C. (1996). Folie et travail: de l'analyse étiologique aux contradictions théoriques [Madness and work: from aetiological analysis to theoretical contradictions], *Psychiatrie française*, 2: 123–140.

Chapter Two—Bensaïd, A. (1990). Apport de la psychopathologie du travail à l'étude d'une bouffée délirante aiguë [What the psychopathology of work can bring to the study of an acute delirious episode] *Archives des maladies professionnelles*, 52: 307–310.

Chapter Three—Doniol-Shaw, G., & Guiho-Bailly, M.-P. (1994) Emploi, conditions de travail et santé des employées dans les services [Employment, working conditions and employee health in the service industry]. *Cahiers du Mage*, 4: 15–23.

Chapter Four—Dejours, C. (1996).Centralité du travail et théorie de la sexualité [Centrality of work and sexuality theory]. *Adolescence*, 14: 9–27.

Chapter Five—M. Grenier-Pezé, M. (2008). «La fabrique des harceleurs», *Ils ne mouraient pas tous mais tous étaient frappés*. ["The bully factory", *They didn't all die but they all took a beating*.] *Journal de la consultation «Souffrance et Travail» 1997–2008* ["Suffering and Work": A Clinician's Journal 1997–2008] (pp.11–32). France: Pearson Education.

Chapter Six—Dejours, C. (2005). "Nouvelles formes de servitude et suicide" [New forms of servitude and suicide]. *Travailler, 13*: 53–74.

ABOUT THE EDITOR AND CONTRIBUTORS

Annie Bensaïd is a psychiatrist and psychoanalyst (Association Psychanalytique de France).

Christophe Dejours is a former hospital practitioner in psychiatry, a psychoanalyst and Professor of the Chair of Psychoanalysis, Health and Work at France's Conservatoire National des Arts et Métiers (National Conservatory of Arts and Crafts). He is a psychoanalyst-member of the Association Psychanalytique de France and the Institut de Psychosomatique de Paris (the Paris Psychosomatic Institute).

Marie Grenier-Pezé is a Doctor of Psychology, a psychoanalyst and expert to the Versailles Court of Appeal. "Suffering and Work" Surgery, Nanterre Centre d'Accueil et de Soins Hospitaliers, (Welcome Centre and Hospital Care).

Marie-Pierre Guiho-Bailly is a psychiatrist-psychoanalyst and practitioner affiliated with the Angers University Hospital, LEEST (Laboratory for Ergonomics and Epidemiology in Occupational Health), University of Angers.

Patrick Lafond is a former psychiatric nurse and relaxation therapist.

SERIES EDITOR'S FOREWORD

The Publications Committee of the International Psychoanalytical Association continues, with this volume, the series "Psychoanalytic Ideas and Applications".

The aim of this series is to focus on the scientific production of significant authors whose works are outstanding contributions to the development of the psychoanalytic field and to set out relevant ideas and themes, generated during the history of psychoanalysis, that deserve to be known and discussed by present psychoanalysts.

The relationship between psychoanalytic ideas and their applications has to be put forward from the perspective of theory, clinical practice, technique, and research so as to maintain their validity for contemporary psychoanalysis.

The Publication Committee's objective is to share these ideas with the psychoanalytic community and with professionals in other related disciplines, in order to expand their knowledge and generate a productive interchange between the text and the reader.

Psychopathology of Work: Clinical Observations, edited by Christophe Dejours, is an original book that addresses an important but not particularly known subject, that of patients suffering from their relation to work. While work is always subsequently affected in every mental disorder, in this volume six clinical observations are provided to show how work *in itself* can deeply affect individual mental functioning, thus later generating difficulties in other aspects of patients' life. This particular and interesting point of view can actually greatly help all clinicians in the field of psychopathology, and will be of great interest for psychoanalysts as well. Special thanks are therefore due to the editor and to the other four contributors to this volume that enriches this important IPA book series.

Gennaro Saragnano
Series Editor
Chair, IPA Publications Committee

Introduction

Christophe Dejours

This book aims to provide clinicians with certain "observations" relating to the psychopathology of work, namely the accounts of patients whose disorders raise questions over their work situation. As such, the book is neither a treatise, nor even an introduction to the psychopathology of work, as numerous works have already been devoted to this very theme:

Louis Le Guillant, *Quelle psychiatrie pour notre temps?* [*Which Psychiatry for our Times?*], (Érès, 1985)

Paul Sivadon, & Adolfo Fernandez-Zoïla, *Temps de travail et temps de vivre* [*Time for Working and Time for Living*], (Pierre Mardaga, 1996)

Isabelle Billiard, *Santé mentale et travail, l'émergence de la psychopathologie du travail* [*Mental Health and Work, the Emergence of the Psychopathology of Work*], (La Dispute, 2001)

Joseph Torrente, *Le psychiatre et le travailleur* [*The Psychiatrist and the Working Subject*], (Doin, 2004)

Marie-Claire Carpentier-Roy, *Corps et âme: psychopathologie du travail infirmier* [*Body and Soul: the Psychopathology of Nursing*], (Liber, 1995)

Marie-Claire Carpentier-Roy, & Michel Vézina, *Le travail et ses malentendus* [*Work and its Misunderstandings*], (Presses de l'Université Laval, and Toulouse: Octares, 2000)

Pascale Molinier, *Les enjeux psychiques du travail* [*The Psychic Challenges of Work*]. *Introduction à la psychodynamique du travail* [*Introduction to the Psychodynamics of Work*], (Payot «Petite Bibliothèque», 2008)

Christophe Dejours, *Travail, usure mentale* [*Work, the Mental Grind*], (Bayard, 1980 [new expanded edition, 2005]).

What we have chiefly focused upon here are various issues that arise for the practitioner, in the consultation room or at the hospital, when he or she sees a patient who claims their work situation has become intolerable. Is this a persecution syndrome dressed up as a work grievance, or a failure syndrome in disguise? Is the grievance feeding some form of masochism that seeks an obliging witness? At times this is the case, and work, in this instance, is simply the back-drop for a drama that originates elsewhere, in a story that began long before the precipitation of the crisis.

Nevertheless, the opposite conjuncture may also occur: the patient is unquestionably suffering a psychopathological decompensation, but the role that may be traced back to work in the crisis is so ambigu-ous that it may sometimes escape the patient him- or herself. This is indeed the case with the opening two observations of this book. The first consists of an acute somatic decompensation leading to the admis-sion of the patient to intensive care (*status asthmaticus*). In the second, reported by Annie Bensaïd, the patient's persecutory delusions, which lead to hospitalisation, do not connote any relation to work in their subject-matter. Thus nothing in the symptomatology strikes the clini-cian as being work-related. This means that the psychopathology of work is not always obvious from the outset; at times it must be sought out deliberately, as it will not spontaneously present itself to the practitioner.

In the third observation (recounted by Marie-Pierre Guiho-Bailly and Patrick Lafond), chronicling the case of a confusional syndrome, we see particularly clearly how work, in the first instance, serves the patient as an effective mediation in the recovery of her mental health. And we gain an understanding of how, following an organisational restructuring at work, her professional occupation in the second instance becomes deleterious, driving the patient to a rather remarkable psychopathological decompensation suggestive of dementia.

The fourth observation involves a young patient who consults the clinician because of emotional issues that are impacting upon her sexuality. Her analysis shows how work is at once a powerful mediator of self-fulfilment, and the source of conflict relating to her sexual identity. This observation, more so than in the previous cases, demonstrates how the relation to work is intertwined with the sexual economy. The gender dimension was already present in the first two observations, in the form of a type of virility. In high-risk or hazardous trades (such as the construction industry) this virility is called upon to serve collective defensive strategies—strategies necessary to overcome fear and to continue one's work. But in the fourth observation, gender reveals itself as a conflict between virility and muliebrity, eventually leading to a genuine sexual identity disorder. (Muliebrity—from the Latin *muliebris*—refers to forms of behaviour the articulation of which specifically characterises the female condition: discretion, helpfulness, submission, renunciation, and so on.)

Gender once again rears its head in the fifth observation (reported by Marie Grenier-Pezé) in the form of subjugation to "desexualisation" in a female manager working in a male-dominated environment (Mrs T). This observation immediately places work to the front and centre of the grievance and the symptoms leading up to the consultation, in the form of psychological harassment. But in this case, the harassment victim (Solange) goes to see the doctor some months before Mrs T, the middle manager who carried out the bullying against Solange, herself becomes ill and consults the same clinician. This observation is particularly interesting, in that it shows how placing the listening focus specifically on the relation to work enables us to deconstruct the logic of psychological bullying which cannot be reduced to a simplistic account of a sadist and her victim. On the basis of this, it is possible to analyse and to treat the psychopathological disorders; the working through however does not pass through the ordinary channels used in conventional clinical practice.

The sixth observation is devoted to the analysis of a case of suicide at the workplace. Here, unquestionably, the relation to work is instrumental in the victim's suicidal acting-out. But even when injustice and bad treatment are implicated, the psychopathology may still raise doubts over what specifically comes down to work and what comes down in its own right to the patient's character traits or personality structure in the genesis of the decompensation. Is the extremely severe depressive syndrome preceding the suicide due to work alone, primarily due to work, or due only incidentally to work? Evaluating these varying degrees of attribution is not an easy thing to do. In the observation presented here, the various sides of the argument are examined in turn, giving the reader an idea of the difficulties the clinician must face.

Ultimately, in this final observation, as in the five that precede it, it becomes clear that, for the practitioner, the main problem lies in the *aetiology*, namely, in identifying the process involved in the genesis of the decompensation. What is at stake in aetiological investigation is fundamental not only to advances in knowledge in psychopathology, but also to the therapeutic process. The reason being that the care tailored to patients' needs can differ radically depending upon the aetiological diagnosis. And yet, aetiological diagnosis is often impossible in a single patient interview. We must, therefore, acknowledge that, in the first instance, the rational response in clinical practice involves coming to an agreement with the patient over an initial treatment plan: patient and clinician seeking together to understand how events concatenate; and, more specifically, how the patient's efforts to resist decompensation have come unstuck. We must often come to this via the retrospective analysis of preceding periods in the patient's history, when the psychic relation to work was appropriately configured. This has the aim of bringing to light the particular resources and skills that were drawn on by the patient to master his or her relation to work when the situation was more favourable. For when work generates pleasure, this as a rule does not happen merely by chance. To make the most of a satisfactory or favourable working situation, one must still be capable of deftly grasping it with both hands without compromising or squandering it.

These observations have been chosen because they show quite convincingly that without a specifically-oriented focus on work, and without a minimum of knowledge and erudition regarding the working world, we may completely miss the aetiological diagnosis and go on to make mistakes in the treatment approach that would exacerbate the patient's suffering and prolong the illness.

The role of the relation to work in mental disorders, as well as in the construction of health, is much more significant than generally assumed. To put it another way, the relation to work is always involved, both in the construction of mental health and in the genesis of illness. Or, put still another way, the relation to work is never neutral when it comes to mental health. For if work can give rise to the worst, as with the cases presented here, it can also give rise to the best. Through work, many of us find the opportunity to add to our identities and shore up our mental health. Conversely, those who are deprived of work through unemployment are also deprived of the right to make a contribution to their company, their society, even to their culture. And, again, they are deprived of the major rewards of recognition, and to acquire any kind of self-worth, even self-love, it is difficult for the majority of men and women to do without this.

The principal difficulty, in terms of aetiological investigation, lies in managing to distinguish between what comes from work and what comes from the private, indeed the personal spheres, in the aetiology of a decompensation.

This question has already been alluded to above regarding observation number six on a workplace suicide. But, all the same, it is useful to come back to it. If such a division is difficult to make, it is because the categories "work" and "outside-work" are brought into opposition by material and spatial features. But this separation between work and outside-work holds no relevance to psychic life.

Whenever we are obliged to deploy subtle and sound defences, to withstand the pain caused by the pressures of work, these defences engage the entire personality. As such, they have a major impact upon behaviours and attitudes in the private sphere, up to and including the bodily economy and in love relationships. Furthermore, if we take account of the relationships of domination of men over women, or gender relations, the intermeshing of work and private life becomes even more pronounced and complicated. To work in the sphere of production we add the issue of the division of labour in the domestic sphere. And this division in the private sphere is never independent of each and every man and woman's relation to work in the productive sphere.

As soon as the relation to work is undermined by the influence of accumulated pressures, overwork, unfair treatment, harassment, fear or threats of dismissal, the effects on the economy of family relationships with partners and children are considerable. In other words, when the relation to work becomes pathogenic, this frequently results in harmful consequences in the private sphere, in the form of affective conflicts which are then the "knock-on" effects of the deterioration of the work situation. By assigning the decompensation to conflicts in the private sphere, because there are in fact conflicts in the family, we are perhaps making an analytical error in mistaking the effects for the cause.

Conversely, the severe conflicts and pain emerging in the private space often have damaging effects on the capacity for work and on the ability to participate in relations that need to be maintained with others in order to play one's part towards pulling together within a team. Then again, at times it is by means of a powerful investment, even a temporary over-investment in work, that some individuals are able to overcome the deleterious psychic effects of mourning or illness of a loved one.

The elements alluded to in this overview are fragmentary. I have mentioned them here to remind the reader that the separation between work and outside-work is irrelevant from the point of view of psychic functioning. They have been collected together in such a way to suggest that analysis of the subjective relation to work should be carried out in all clinical situations, even when the complaint is not directly related to work, as shown by the first four observations in this volume.

Or, putting it another way and in conclusion to this introduction, the psychopathology of work does not only concern *occupational* physicians and *occupational* psychologists. It deserves to be a tool in the armoury of all clinicians who work in the area of psycho-pathology, even when they do not specialise in the field of work.

Herein lies the aim of this book: simply to raise awareness of the psychopathology of work among practitioners who as yet have little knowledge of it. And for those who are already familiar with it, to enter into enough detail in this clinical study to give some "substance" with which to add depth to the arguments of the aetiological discussion.

CHAPTER ONE

Madness and work: from aetiological analysis to theoretical contradictions (a case of *status asthmaticus*)

Christophe Dejours

Introduction

W hether we like it or not, we must face the fact that the theoretical and clinical questions raised by the impact of the pressures of professional life on mental health remain poorly understood by psychiatrists. We all know, vaguely, that somewhere there is a stream of research going on known as the "psychopathology of work". But few know any more than this. How many of us have heard of Louis Le Guillant (1985), how many can recall the content of studies carried out by the French League of Mental Hygiene, have read the research on work by Claude Veil (1952, 1964), or know of the theorisations of Adolfo Fernandez-Zoïla (1979, 1988) on the experience of work? We have all, in other respects, heard the whispers about research on work-related stress, or "burn-out" (Cherniss, 1980), probably in the media or news weeklies more than through professional journals, as it so happens, but we hardly raise an eyebrow. Because this stream of research unfolds within a behaviourist framework: accessible to the human resources directors and other administrators, certainly, but a little too succinct and simplistic for the practitioner who wishes to explore the psychopathological or aetiological argument.

The subjective relation to work plays a key role in the processes involved both in the construction of health as well as in psychiatric and psychosomatic decompensation. Work cannot be held solely to account for a socially generated discontent, one that lies at the root of all somatic afflictions (medical toxicology) and the most vicious mental afflictions (alienation). The mental damage inflicted by unemployment is there to suggest otherwise. But it would be a mistake to simply make use of this new psychopathology to justify a blissful apologia for labour according to which good health would come only "through toil".

For all that, the conflicting data presented by clinical experience of happy and unhappy relations to work should not discourage the psychopathologist. These contradictions are understandable. For some researchers in psychology, in anthropology, in sociology, and in economics, work occupies a central place in the functioning of society, the production of wealth and national economies, as well as in psychic functioning and the construction of identity. The "centrality of work" is the expression by which, in the scientific community, we refer to the thesis held by these authors (de Bandt et al., 1995).

Psychopathology offers compelling arguments in favour of this thesis. Work is nowhere near to being replaced by substitute investments. Those with plenty of free time are primarily in temporary or precarious work situations, or they are unemployed, and it is not at all clear whether they derive any substantial benefits vis-à-vis the struggle for good health. It would seem, rather, that the scarcity or the deprivation of activity and remunerated employment makes their relation to good health more precarious.

In no way do we share the theories on the end of work, which are of little more use than theorising about the end of history. But we should recognise their powerful impact on the *Zeitgeist* and the formation of perspectives: not only those of the wider population, but of scientists themselves. The widely held social refusal of work filters down to exert its influence upon psychiatrists themselves, who are left somewhat at a loss to explain the discrepancy between the vision of unemployment, poverty, job insecurity, and so on, offered up to them through their day-to-day analytic experience, and what they have been promised by triumphant discourse, heralding the "end of work" as Western civilisation enters into the "age of freedom".

The scant interest afforded by psychopathologists to the centrality of work is due in part, also naturally, to other causes that materialise before the job crisis. It would be impossible to cover all of these in this chapter. And yet, if the analysis of them was familiar to practitioners, perhaps it would lead to a movement of curiosity for the psychopathology and the psychodynamics of work, which in turn may have significant consequences on the practice of psychiatry. The principal difficulty, however, will not be overcome any time soon. It resides in the fact that work is an enigma that is as opaque as the unconscious. As with the aforementioned unconscious, any psychiatrist has some experience of work. But between the experience of the unconscious and the conceptualisation of this experience, there is a step that can cost several years on the divan. The formulation of the experience of work, which is first and foremost the experience of society to the point of the purpose or function of one's own self and body, is also a difficult matter. And yet each of us has this experience, as suggested by the theory of Ignace Meyerson (1948), which was once again taken up and questioned by Fernandez-Zoïla (1996), for whom work is a psychological function. A clinical mine of inestimable wealth exists, but has not been exploited by ordinary psychiatry.

This chapter is aimed at those who have an intuition of the "centrality of work" and who would like to have an idea of what clinical data on the subjective relation to work may reveal to us.

In order to do so, we shall draw upon one observation. Although this form of decompensation is fairly common, the discussion of its aetiology is complex. To attempt an approach, even schematically, we will first require at our disposal certain conceptual elements of work psychodynamics. Then, we shall move on to the account of the case of Mr A and a discussion of the aetiology of the decompensation from a psychoanalytic and psychosomatic viewpoint. Finally, we shall outline the implications of these two aetiological analyses on the management of the treatment. This will then give us a number of strands in our reflection upon the following question: how is it that two aetiopathogenic theories that are so contrasting, even contradictory, can both be right at the same time?

Work and fear

The example we shall draw upon is taken from the construction industry. One of the characteristics of work in this sector, in relation to other work situations in industry or the service sector, is the significance of accident risk. While much has been made of the consequences of these working conditions upon the health of the body, less attention has been paid to the impact of exposure to risk on the psychological state of these workers. And yet they adopt behaviours that should arouse our curiosity; particularly in relation to prevention and safety. To this they frequently counter a kind of passive resistance, and at times demonstrate a clear unwillingness to respect safety guidelines and to cooperate with health and safety specialists. Is there not a paradox here? How is it that the community hardest hit by workplace accidents is opposed to measures specifically intended to protect it?

If we take a closer look, we see that, for these same workers, disregard for rules and disorder are not only common practice, but are *positively connoted* as external signs of courage. Over and above the resistance to health and safety, these workers display a certain taste for showy displays of muscle strength, agility, even physical prowess. Worse still, at times they artificially add to the existing site risks by organising kinds of bravery contests, through a variety of tests of strength, skill, and courage. These contests are an integral part of the day-to-day working life. They take on a more dramatic form when, on to the site, comes a new worker. They move on to shows of force, but in doing this they also test the newcomer, going as far as compelling him to take part in what are essentially obstacle courses. Either the applicant conforms to these worksite conventions, or he becomes the subject of taunts, and soon after excluded—even harassed—until he quits the job and leaves the site. The denunciation of the deviant is accompanied by disqualification that often takes the pejorative form of accusations according to which the offender behaves like a woman, even like a "fag" and so on. In the community of these workers, they cultivate a particular penchant for disputes to be settled "man to man", that is to say, by using fists if necessary. *Conserere manus* is a type of behaviour that itself has connotations of virility.

What is more, all of these behaviours are articulated with a sexually specific *discourse*. Courage, strength, recklessness, and rule-breaking are on the side of the *virile*. Conversely, complaining of any kind is prohibited, even when in pain. Showing any interest whatsoever in the health of one's body or mental health is forbidden, as is expressing fear, or for that matter showing too much of a taste for caution, looking a bit too closely at work safety and risk prevention.

Complaining, anxiety, and hesitance—these are attitudes that are denounced as being typically effeminate.

The penchant for alcoholic drinks is easily understood in this context as these facilitate sociability and conviviality between men, and therefore the cohesion of the group. But above all, alcohol possesses a powerful anxiolytic action—an action that furthermore is perfectly *dissimulated*. Alcohol is a substrate that has all of the qualities of a drug to keep virility intact and one that is able to fight fear.

We therefore find ourselves before a system that combines:

1. reticence towards and disregard for health and safety

2. dangerous risk-taking behaviour

3. strict discipline towards the external signs of courage

4. any allusion to fear or pain is strictly forbidden

5. a discourse that calibrates all behaviours, attitudes, and conducts in relation to a virility/femininity grid.

This seemingly paradoxical system reveals its coherence when it becomes clear that these workers are in truth tormented by fear, by very virtue of the fact of their exposure to accident risk.

Now this fear, if experienced without dissimulation, would quite simply be incompatible with the continuation of work as it is organised in a real-life setting, on major construction sites. And for this reason these workers are driven to construct the defensive system as described, the mission of which is precisely to fight against the conscious perception of fear.

The concept of the defensive strategy and the question of normality

I will not enter into the internal mechanisms of functioning of these behaviours here. Instead I shall, for now, confine myself to identifying them as *defensive strategies* (Dejours, 1980), intended to combat the psychic pain brought about by working in a climate of threat.

I shall especially emphasise the *key functional value* of this defensive strategy of construction workers. We see that it has undeniable disadvantages, insofar as it interferes with health and safety campaigns, contributes in some way to a resistance to change, and may even at times add additional risks to the existing danger, particularly during these collective contests of courage and bravery, occasionally resulting in accidents that are quick to be condemned. And yet, evidently it is vital to grasp the practical necessity of these paradoxical behaviours. Without them, the organisation of the work and the objective pressures of the site would be humanly unsustainable.

The avoidance of the pejorative judgement, so often passed by supervisory staff and the layperson regarding these supposedly aberrant behaviours, does not constitute a difficulty for the psychiatrist accustomed to moving in diverse sectors of society and not conceding to reactive emotional or social reactions.

The difficulty for the psychiatrist lies elsewhere. If he succeeds in suspending judgement, he will not easily manage to keep himself from tending to make psychopathological diagnoses in the face of any human behaviour as soon as it is submitted for his opinion.

These behaviours of bravado, indiscipline, provocation, insolence, risk-taking, and tobacco or alcohol dependence: one would need to be able to recognise them without immediately considering them to be signs of irresponsibility, stupidity, immaturity, an archaic mentality, or of a psychopathological or delinquent personality type. Not that there are not, among construction workers, a few psychopaths, but rather because these diagnoses are based on knowledge referential to *psychopathology* and not to the *psychodynamics* of "normality". It is clearly outside the scope of this chapter to deal with the meaning that may be ascribed to normality, in clinical practice, but it is, however, useful to point out that this concept has occupied a central role in the psychodynamics of work since 1980.

Many psychiatrists, certainly, consider themselves to know what normality is once they have gained some clinical experience and a theoretical understanding of madness. And yet, the psychodynamics of work (the clinical experience and the theory of "normality" in a work situation) cannot be superimposed on to the classic psychopathology of work (the work of Louis Le Guillant (1963) and Jean Bégoin (1957)), in that it is first and foremost a psychological study of *ordinary* situations, where people manage to stave off mental illness, and not the study of extraordinary mental decompensation. Psychoanalysis, which brings into question the conventional departure between mental illness and normality, is surely the royal road to a re-framing of a psychodynamics of normality. But it cannot act as a theory of normality.

Normality is a conquest and the "strategies" deployed to maintain it are unknown both to psychiatry and to psychoanalysis. In medicine just as in psychiatry, there is a tendency to apprehend normality, indeed good health, using *negative concepts*: the absence of illness, the silence of the organs, and so on. This is a flawed conception. The health of the body is the result of the relentless struggle (if we may use this metaphor) between physiological regulations and physicochemical-biological disturbances. It is quite another thing to a negatively characterised passive state of absence of illness. The same is true, it would seem, for mental health. Here also, very sophisticated "regulations" exist, mobilising intersubjective dynamics not only in the affective field (which psychoanalysis recognises) but also in the field of social relationships and civil connections, overlooked by psychoanalysis, which examine in particular the sociology and anthropology of health, but also the psychodynamics of work.

The same behaviour does not have the same meaning depending upon whether it is structured around a sophisticated strategy of struggle for good health or whether is it inscribed within a syndrome of psychopathological decompensation.

This is not a mere technicality, as this is not just a question of analytical perspective. This has to do with two *radically different* functional vocations. In one case, the consumption of alcohol is a powerful, effective, and appropriate means of coping with the pressures of the workplace without going mad. In the other, the consumption of alcohol if anything reveals the overwhelming of the psychoneurotic defences, a sign of the precariousness of the psychosomatic economy, and contributes to the deterioration of the patient's mental and somatic state.

Normality or pathology? The comprehensive approach

How do we know whether this behaviour falls within one dynamic or within the other? There is unfortunately no way to make the distinction, from the outside. Only the subject individually, or workers collectively, may point us in the right direction to follow in our interpretation.

Provided, that is, that the clinicians are able to understand. To do this, they must not only refrain from any judgement, as we have seen above, but must also suspend their knowledge, their understanding, and their presuppositions. Not that clinicians should renounce these and abandon them entirely—quite the opposite—but they should put them on hold while listening to what the "subject of work" has to say.

Thus the first methodological implication of the psychodynamics of work is to advocate in favour of an *understanding* (*Verstehen*) approach—one that we owe to the social sciences and not to the human sciences practitioners (which remains one of history's incongruities, but one that we must come to terms with all the same!).

According to this approach, any behaviour, any posture, any discourse within work, even when seemingly the most aberrant to the outside observer, even when they are redolent of pathological syndromes to the specialised clinician, are deemed rational in relation to good health, as a first-line treatment, whenever they are not the work of isolated personalities. They possess a rationality, indeed a legitimacy, in the sense that these behaviours generally have a precise function in the economy of the subject (or subjects) vis-à-vis the real pressures of work, in their effort to remain within *normality*.

By "an understanding approach or process" we mean that, as the fundamental aim of investigation, the researcher or clinician seeks to investigate what meaning these behaviours and discourses hold *for the operators* before deciding what meaning they hold for the researcher (Alfred Schütz, 1987).

To access the meaning that a certain type of behaviour holds for the subject presupposes that the researcher or clinician must renounce any role as expert and any pronouncement of a diagnosis from the analysis of objective external signs. The understanding approach is resolutely subjectivist (even if the stage of validity testing of the meaning—uncovered by this procedure—in the *après coup*, endeavours to objectivise the status of it). "Neither judge, nor expert", is therefore the maxim we might advance to the psychiatrist focusing on the "centrality of work".

The notion of the collective: from the collective strategy to the construction of the working collective

Another point I would like to emphasise is the *construction* of these defensive strategies. First of all to underscore that these behaviours are not spontaneously occurring, but undergo symbolic elaboration.

This complex system of defence against fear is the result of a *collective* construction and not an individual one. The strategy we have just described is produced by groups of workers, but it is also stabilised, controlled, and maintained *collectively*. The example of young workers or apprentices is illuminating in this regard. Not only does each have to accept these trials organised by the group, but the newcomer must also have something to bring to the table. Conversely, if someone does not subscribe to the defensive strategy, he single-handedly becomes, through his "timorous" behaviour, a threat to the stability of the defensive strategy and ergo to the psychic equilibrium of the other workers. It is because of this group dimension that these strategies are known as "collective defence strategies".

I will add that not only are these strategies constructed by the group, but beyond this they contribute in an essential, fundamental, indeed a foundational, way to the construction and the stabilisation of the *working collective*. It is because they share the collective defence strategy and the rigour that goes along with it that there is recognition between workers as members of the group, and they are able to establish relationships of trust and solidarity between each other.

Finally, I will note that at times there occurs a kind of perversion, if I may use this term—to be taken here strictly prosaically. A kind of perversion, thus, of the collective defence strategy, which we term "defensive ideology of work practice". This "perversion" appears when workers idealise the defensive strategy, this in turn acquiring an inflexible rigidity such that it may no longer be discussed or criticised. Workers risk becoming the victims of this, insofar as the defensive ideology becomes impregnable and prevents any change—even positive change—to the relation to work, to organisational pressures, and to risks. But we shall leave the "ideologies" and come back to the "strategies".

Accordingly there exists a whole range of collective defence strategies, which is in every instance specific to the work situation. If we go even further into detail, we may show that *pain*, the defensive strategies against which tend to take on the role of mental control, is always closely bound up with the *organisational* constraints of work. Put another way, the entire field of mental health at work refers to the organisation of work, while physical health refers above all to working conditions.

Suffering at work and mental health (in the order of the individual)

What are the consequences of these collective defence strategies on the psychic economy and the mental equilibrium of these workers? It can be shown that suffering with work as its source penetrates the private space and the innermost thoughts of every one of us, and so touches the very "material" offered up to the psychiatrist's clinical investigation.

Mr A is Algerian. He is a little over forty years old. He does not know his exact date of birth. He has worked in construction in France for around fifteen years. His wife must be approximately thirty-eight to forty years old, and he has had six children with her, the oldest of whom is twenty and the youngest eighteen months. The only working member of the family, he must meet the needs of nine people: his six children, his wife, his mother-in-law, and himself. He earns less than €1,000 per month. He leaves the house every morning at 5.45 a.m. and returns in the evenings at around 8.15 p.m.

For approximately the last two years, he has begun to suffer from nocturnal dyspnoea. For the last two months, he has no longer been sleeping at night because of the aggravation of this dyspnoea. A few days ago, on the worksite, he triggered an acute severe asthma exacerbation.

The interview with this patient was somewhat difficult owing to significant difficulties in his command of French. This is a man who to all appearances is rather friendly, with an easy smile, and who seems eager to cooperate. He does not understand what is happening to him; over the last few months he has lost around fifteen kilos. He is deeply upset by this new illness that is stripping him of his ability to work. He says he is not depressed, but he emphasises the fact that he no longer has any courage to work. He no longer has any strength or desire to go out to the building site; he has lost his drive, and his lack of courage is quite clearly, for him, the sign that he "is no longer a man" and that he is unwell.

The issue, from the psychopathological point of view, lies in understanding why this asthma appeared suddenly two years ago. To ask the patient, it would appear that no event, no specific circumstance, no particular condition in his mental, affective, professional, or material life can be pinpointed during the period preceding the first appearance of this illness or concomitant to its onset. For lack of the patient's associations as our focus, upon the links he does not make, in any case, between somatic events and psychic events, we might be tempted to confine ourselves to seeking an organic aetiology for this asthma: an occupational aetiology for example. It is, therefore, by conducting a relatively directional investigation, in seeking to reconstruct a biography or at least a sequence of events that we gradually find ourselves in a position to advance a construct on the aetiopathogenesis of his affliction.

Since 1971, Mr A had sought to bring his wife and children to France. Without success. It was impossible to get an apartment in an H.L.M. (*Habitation à Loyer Modéré* or low rent housing). For years then, he works doggedly, by himself, saving up. He lives in makeshift premises and makeshift shelters on construction sites with a handful of colleagues who are in the same situation as he is. A community of men. During this period, he does not suffer from a single somatic symptom, or from any psychoneurotic symptom. Two years ago, he finally managed to get accommodation through a "friend". Or rather, by means of a large sum of money to a well-connected compatriot at the S. Town Hall who acquires for him, as if by a miracle, an "F4" (a four-roomed, or two-bedroom, apartment).

He then brings his wife over and she immediately falls pregnant with his child, who is now approximately eighteen months old. The patient makes no connection between the two things and yet the dates match up perfectly: the asthma began during the period in which his wife came to join him in France. It is impossible to find any severe conflict situations with the patient's wife, either because he is concealing them, or simply because there are none. If anything, when he talks of his wife, he clearly shows great tenderness and genuine affection. This marriage is not the result of a parental "inter-family" arrangement. When he first met his wife, they chose each other mutually, and the mere mention of this time in his life has his face aglow with happiness and smiles, accompanied by a certain embarrassment and some shyness in bringing up such thoughts in front of a doctor.

I try, as much as is possible, to get him to talk about his wife and children. Two of his children remained in Algeria, with Mr A's mother-in-law. The youngest four are with their mother and with Mr A. When I talk to him about his children's health, he expresses himself animatedly. Clearly, he shows great deal of focused concern for his children's well-being, unusually so it seems to me, in this context.

When I ask him if his life was easier before or after the arrival of his wife, he immediately replies that life is much more enjoyable now that she is here. Previously, he explains, it was hard for him as he only heard from his wife and children every so often; he did not know if they were healthy or if they were unwell. Since their arrival, he concerns himself over their health, and he finds it reassuring to have them close to him so he can take care of them and his wife. However, it is indeed since their arrival that the patient has been suffering from respiratory impairment.

This is how we can interpret the psychopathological history of this patient. Until the arrival of his family, this man established a relationship of control over fear, illness, and bodily states, which was mediated by the collective defence strategies of his fellow workers on the building site. But during this entire period he only ever lived with other men, in the temporary shelters on the worksites; men who, like him, shared the occupational risks and collective defence strategies. Throughout this phase of his existence, life outside work (that is to say, his private sphere) was concordant and complementary to the defensive economy vis-à-vis the pressures of work.

Investment of the professional sphere vs. investment of the private sphere

However, when his wife and children arrive, everything changes. Why? By questioning the patient, I discover a family economy quite different to what clinical experience ordinarily reveals. More often than not, we hear allusions to a life essentially occupied by work, while free time is spent outside the family: in cafes, in male company, playing dominos for example, or some or other political, associative, cultural, or social activity, but always without the spouse and without the children. Time spent at home is therefore reduced to the minimum, and the man pays but a fleeting interest in the lives and in the concerns of his family members. Any matters relating to school, health, running the home, and all the domestic tasks are, generally, entrusted to the wife and the older daughters. So the man often demonstrates a great deal of unawareness, even slight disinterest, in the comings and goings of home life.

This type of economy of intersubjective relations in the affective and familial sphere, and in a broader sense in the private space, is not the result of a simple "cultural conformism" particular to North Africans for example; we find this just as much in civil construction workers in Brazil as those in construction and civil engineering in France. It is instead the result of a successful articulation between the logic of the collective defence strategy and the defensive virility against fear at the worksite, on the one hand, and the organisation of relationships in the private space, on the other, in such as way as to ensure that continuity is thus established and maintained. Manly, even macho, at the worksite, he also displays his virility in private behaviours, inasmuch as partners in the private space tolerate or are prepared to engage with it (which is not always the case; but then family crisis is inevitable).

In other words, these behaviours of construction workers at home are the result of an alignment, indeed a "technical solidarity" (to borrow here from Nicolas Dodier, 1995), in the man's endeavours to remain within the limits of the collective defence strategies. Anything related to health, illness, suffering, pain, the body, blood, accidents, and so on; he, the man who works, is somehow spared by his entourage.

Thus, through the intervention of defensive dynamics, we find the embodiment of what, in sociological terms, we mean by the expression: the articulation, coordination, and coherence between relations of *production* (work) and relations of *reproduction* (family).

But in the case of Mr A we discover something else entirely. Where I was looking for conflict—even violence—between him and his wife, (or towards his children), which is commonplace, I discover instead that Mr A enjoys a good relationship with his wife, whom he truly loves. I am rather surprised by this, as this is not all that common in North African families, where marriages are often arranged by the parents for social and commercial reasons. I ask him for some clarifications, so discovering that this was not so for him. It was he who made the acquaintance of his wife in his late teens, immediately falling in love with her. They were in love with each other and it was together that they decided to get married—and they love each other still.

Whenever he has a free moment, Mr A returns home to spend time with his family. He loves his children, he cares about their studies even if he is unable to help them, and he is particularly conscious of their health. He keeps a close watch on their health and willingly takes them to the doctor whenever he is able to take a day off work, and so on.

It is this relation to the health, sickness and suffering of his family members that is quite unusual in this type of worker. Indeed, to lavish such attention upon the health of his children, one must, mentally, be in a position to be able to identify with them, with their suffering, their needs, and so on. To identify with them means being able to put himself in their place. Now, putting himself in their place is not very compatible with the collective defence strategy aimed precisely at putting completely out of mind any evocation of the illness and/or suffering of the body.

For Mr A, the arrival of his wife and children constitutes a stark break between the defences against suffering at work and what this brings with it, and the patient's existential choices in his private space and in his domestic life. Now, the affective investment seems to be the stronger. Others would have perhaps coped by generating a situation of conflict in the family and by fleeing the family home, only returning to eat and sleep, even escaping family life entirely or divorcing. But he, Mr A, holds on fast to his family life; it is on the work side that his situation becomes destabilised. All of a sudden, he feels drained, all his courage gone, he can no longer push through, he says. He who, up to then, had been a valued worker, now starts to get into trouble. He can no longer stand himself in this situation. He is no longer well-liked by his bosses. Then he starts to suffer from asthmatiform dyspnoea.

By the time I see him, Mr A is hospitalised in intensive care, with *status asthmaticus*.

Thus I shall stop here to underline this point, which is in my view significant. Namely that the defensive strategies required to withstand the pathogenic pressures of the organisation of work function only at the sites of work. The theoretical cut-off between work space and outside-work space is entirely artificial. By leaving the worksite, the subject is still himself, he cannot change skin nor change his psychic economy. This means that suffering at work, by summoning up specific defensive strategies, will distort the subject's entire mental organisation, its tentacles reaching as far as relationships with children and partners. The economy of love and the erotic economy are in some ways taken over by work relations. If the private space is resistant, if it is not compatible with the defensive demands of work, we should be prepared for decompensation. Thus, from this example, we should keep in mind that there is a *fundamental psychic solidarity between work life and outside-work life, or a unity of economy between the two existential modalities.*

This problem is not specific to migrant workers in unskilled positions in the construction industry. I have observed exactly the same thing in *fighter pilots*. As long as they are young bachelors, they often bear up well to occupational risks. But marriage, and particularly the birth of children, are one of the most frequent causes of what, in the air force, is termed "unfit for duties as a fighter pilot". They must then be reclassified as instructors in flight schools, as helicopter pilots, or as pilots in military air transport, or even suspend them. That is to say, they must remove them from the risky situations they formerly coped with so well or even prized highly. We meet with exactly the same issues with executives and directors.

The problem is the same with Mr A. If he can be reclassified in an occupation without the routine risks of the construction industry, then he will fare better and perhaps be cured. This is at least what is suggested by the progress made by Mr A who, since that time, has been able to change jobs, becoming an assistant in a small business, and no longer suffers from asthma.

Theoretical-clinical remarks

The next point I should like to emphasise specifically is that a large part of the consequences of mental suffering at work does not always manifest itself at the workplace. In striving to hold on to their position, some workers destroy their family life, and it is not uncommon for the children to ultimately suffer from mental disorders, the connections to the parent's suffering being very easy to elucidate. But rarely is this done in standard psychiatric practice, due to a lack of knowledge among the majority of our psychiatrist colleagues as far as the psychodynamics of work is concerned.

Finally, I would like to touch upon the question of the symptomatic form of Mr A's decompensation. Why asthma? Other subjects, placed in analogous psychological circumstances, would not suffer from asthma but instead a work accident followed by a post-traumatic syndrome, others from depression, and others again from delirious episode (Annie Bensaïd, 1990).

This means only that the semiological form of the decompensation does not depend upon the pressures of work that are at the very beginning of this crisis. The semiological form depends upon the subject's mental organisation, his or her past, childhood, parental relationships, and so on. Even a person's genetics, some psychiatrists would say. It is therefore important to note that, as long as we stay this side of the decompensation, work inscribes highly specific marks upon the subject's defensive organisation. But once decompensation has occurred, if we take it in isolation from its context, it is impossible to clearly recover the traces of the organisation of work that was nonetheless at the very beginning of the crisis.

With regard to Mr A, decompensation took the form of a life-threatening acute somatisation. The reasons for this vulnerability to somatisation we shall not discuss here, as they would lead us too far into the terrain of psychosomatics. Nevertheless, it is indeed by taking action regarding his work that Mr A's psychosomatic problem could be resolved. Even after it had reached hospitalisation stage! Indeed, it was only because the conventional intensive care technologies were rendered ineffective for several days that the psychiatrist needed to be called. During the course even of the initial investigation, despite the difficult conditions often encountered in "liaison psychiatry", the patient's somatic state improved: his heart rate decreased, his breathing improved, and so on, giving the psychiatric intervention the appearance of a "miracle". In fact, it rather seems that the sedation of the patient's anxiety and the improvement of his biological variables may have been contemporaneous to the intersubjective dynamic mobilised by the elaborative work on his experience of suffering at work.

Conclusion

At the end of this quick excursion into the clinical presentation of a common decompensation, we find ourselves faced with two types of "causalities" or "causal pathways" (Anne Fagot-Largeault, 1986) that are really quite different and contradictory to each other. The decompensation indeed may be described in two ways:

1.   Our point of departure can either be the analysis of the processes mobilised in favour of the struggle *for good health* (and their being severely compromised by the arrival of the family) thus enabling

an interpretation of the decompensation in relation to the destabilisation of the economy of health. But this analysis only goes as far as the decompensation. Beyond this, the semiological form of the illness leads us to determinants escaping its functional scope.

2. Or, conversely, we may describe the *bio-* and *psychopathological* processes resulting from the decompensation from the medical/ biological data and/or the psychosomatic and infantile characteristics of the patient. But we cannot, then, understand why the decompensation occurred only now nor why the psychosomatic territory, which is fragile and vulnerable to traumatism of all kinds, has thus far *resisted* all the sources of traumatism he would have come up against until the age of thirty-eight to forty years old (i.e., the processes involved in good health).

In this way might the psychosomatic decompensation go by two starkly contrasting "descriptions" (using Elizabeth Anscombe's meaning of the concept). But is this merely a conflict of description, better yet a conflict of interpretation (Paul Ricœur, 1969)? It would appear that the conflict of interpretation here overlays a *duality of substance*. To wit, the initial description would pertain to the processes involved in the construction of health, whereas the second would relate to the processes involved in illness. Herein lies a major contradiction, nonetheless difficult to grasp and accept intellectually: health and sickness may not constitute one and the same process and may not even be contiguous processes, but two qualitatively and objectively divergent sets that do not overlap. Doctors and psychiatrists are familiar with and document illness and the fight against illness. Sociologists and anthropologists have an understanding of the processes involved in the construction of health and in the undermining of this construct.

In this way decompensation can (as much as normality, for that matter) produce two descriptions that do not overlap. Accordingly, a substantial *dualism* would exist between health/illness; not a continuum between the two types of process. This is a dualism which would be reiterated by the scientific dualism between the medical/biological sciences and the social sciences regarding health matters.

Ideally, to render an exhaustive account of a psychosomatic state (normal or pathological) it would be necessary to provide two descriptions: one with regard to the state of the morbid processes, the other with regard to the state of the beneficial processes.

From the therapeutic point of view, it is clear that the analysis of the two types of processes (illness and health) variously suggests markedly different practical measures. In general, however, the approach via only one of the two access routes may be enough to restore an adequate psychosomatic state. But not always. As the example of Mr A shows, his psychosomatic state resisted the practical measures directed against illness, but was receptive to the practical measures directed towards health.

So must we perhaps conclude that the aetiological contradictions remain, for all that we believe the two competing interpretations to be mutually exclusive. The contradiction is if anything lessened should we apprehend the substantial dualism between sickness/health (which incidentally encompasses in large part the dualism of Freud's later drive theory of 1920) suggesting that the two interpretations can be right simultaneously.

The psychodynamics of work possesses the particular characteristic of providing access to the apprehension of certain processes involved in health and in normality. The ideal, however, would be to harness the knowledge in both the fields of health (the psychodynamics of work) and illness (general psychopathology), because then the therapeutic pathways open to the practitioner would increase dramatically.

References

Bégoin, J. (1957). *La névrose des téléphonistes et des mécanographes*. Thesis, Faculté de Médecine de Paris.

Bensaïd, A. (1990). «Apport de la psychopathologie du travail à 1'étude d'une bouffée délirante aiguë. Communication Journées Nationales de Médecine du Travail. Rouen». *Archives des Maladies Professionnelles* (pp. 307–310). Paris: Masson.

Cherniss, C. (1980). *Staff Burnout: Job Stress with Human Services*. Beverly Hills, CA: Sage.

De Bandt, J., Dubar, C., Dejours, C., Gadea, C., & Teiger, C. (1995). *La France malade du travail*. Paris: Bayard.

Dejours, C. (1980). *Travail et usure mentale. Essai de psychopathologie du travail*. Paris: Le Centurion [fifth expanded edition, 2015].

Dodier, N. (1995). *Les hommes et les machines*. Paris: Métailié.

Fagot-Largeault, A. (1986). «Approche médicale de la causalité dans les systèmes complexes». *Archives Internationales de physiologie et de biochimie, 94*: 85–94.

Fernandez-Zoïla, A. (1979). *Rupture de vie et névroses: la maladie langage post-traumatique*. Toulouse: Privat.

Fernandez-Zoïla, A. (1988). «Pour une théorie de l'homme en psychopathologie du travail». In: C. Dejours (Ed.), *Plaisir et souffrance dans le travail, tome I* (pp. 53–75). Paris: AOCIP-CNRS.

Fernandez-Zoïla, A. (1996). «Ignace Meyerson et la psychologie». In: Y. Clot (Ed.), *Histoire de la psychologie du travail*. Toulouse: Octares.

Le Guillant, L. (1963). «Incidences psychopathologiques de la condition de *bonne à tout faire"»*. *L'évolution psychiatrique, 28*: 1–64.

Le Guillant, L. (1985). *Quelle psychiatrie pour notre temps? (Which Psychiatry for our Times?)*. Toulouse: Érès.

Meyerson, I. (1948). *Les fonctions psychologiques et les œuvres*. Paris: Vrin [reprinted 1995, Paris: Albin Michel].

Ricœur, P. (1969). *Le conflit des interprétations (essai d'herméneutique)*. Paris: Seuil.

Schütz, A. (1987). *Le chercheur et le quotidien (phénoménologie des sciences sociales)*. Paris: Méridiens-Klincksieck.

Veil, C. (1952). *La fatigue industrielle et l'organisation du travail*. Doctoral thesis. Faculté de médecine de Paris.

Veil, C. (1964). *Hygiène mentale du travailleur*. Paris: Le François.

CHAPTER TWO

What the psychopathology of work can bring to the study of an acute delirious episode

Annie Bensaïd

This study is devoted to a clinical case analysed in the light of the psychopathology of work. This discipline, such as is our premise, may help in the understanding, indeed the treatment, of some psychiatric decompensation.

In the history of M.S., a construction worker, two types of differentiated pressures become apparent:

1. On the one hand, the pressures engendered by social relationships and the organisation of work. His psychic adaptation to such pressures brings into play a defensive ideology of the building trade echoing back to the working collective;
2. On the other hand, the pressures engendered by the intersubjective relationships within his family, involving defences referring to the subjective order.

In time, between these two types of defensive strategies, insoluble contradictions arise that might play a decisive role in breakdowns of psychic equilibrium. I shall attempt to show how analysis of these defences has had an impact on therapeutic orientation in a way that could not have been conceived without reference to the psychopathology of work.

M.S. is a forty-year-old man who I see in the emergency room at the request of a general practitioner for persecutory-type delusional symptomatology with interpretative and hallucinatory mechanisms, which had developed over the past three months. He had spontaneously consulted a doctor of his own accord a fortnight ago, as he felt like he was "going crazy". Until then, M.S. had never before sought medical attention, much less psychiatric help.

He presents from the outset as a warm, friendly man and relates his difficulties without any reticence even though persecution is at the centre of his current problem-complex. He therefore interacts well despite major anxiety, which manifests itself as logorrhea and shaking of his hands and feet. Certainly alcohol toxicity is present, a recent symptom, he says. And indeed, he does not present any bodily habitus of chronic intoxication (biological assessment carried out some time later will confirm this).

His request is clear: other than seeking reassurance on the risk of him being crazy, he wishes to live a "quiet life with his family".

Of Moroccan origin, and alone in France for seventeen years, he works as a painter in construction. His history of psychopathology began one year before the arrival of his wife and daughters in France. For some months, M.S. has been irritable, nervous—both at the workplace and at home—and violent towards his wife, whom he beats. He regrets this behaviour, cries and consumes alcohol for anxiolytic purposes.

At the same time, certain ideas of reference have been developing: he has the feeling of being followed, watched on the street, on the train that takes him to work, where he is convinced they are talking about him. He thinks that his neighbours and his apartment superintendent are watching him. During that time, he would be called to interview by the district social worker, following an alert by the apartment caretaker on account of the violence he inflicts upon his family. It would then be concluded that M.S. exhibits the symptoms of alcoholism, within a context of the *classic* adaptive difficulties of North African immigrants, presenting a particular risk to his children. Child protection measures will be discussed, a measure frequently used in standard psychiatric practice (note that, within the context of this particular interpretation of M.S.'s pathological behaviour, it is remarkable that the management initially proposed by a female doctor did not incur any particular difficulty).

The cause of his disorder is thus brought back to his immigrant status, indeed to a pre-existing structure (a paranoid personality structure) without reference to work matters, particularly the organisation of work. This is a lack of understanding that does not sit easily with him, as he himself knows that he has changed (he has had no adaptation problems for the last seventeen years), to the point that he no longer recognises himself. He is anxious and withdrawn at work; for the first time ever he gets into a fight at a worksite.

Three months before this initial consultation, he had a work accident: he falls off some scaffolding. His fall was broken when he landed on a balcony, three floors below—without sustaining any injury. He did not take any time off work to avoid getting deeper into financial difficulties, but the following week he would exhibit sleep disturbances in the form of nightmares with nightly flashbacks to this traumatic event, a resurgence of anxiety, irritability, and ideas of reference.

It is within this context that his acoustic-verbal hallucinations would develop: he hears voices—uniquely male—that insult him, call him a coward, and hurl abuse at his wife who is nothing but a *slut*, a *whore*, and that *tell him to divorce her*.

He is completely taken over by his hallucinations, first of all on the train, which frequently forces him to get off before his station; then at the workplace where he continually breaks off what he doing to check *who is talking*, and finally at home.

Feeling threatened, he barricades himself in his house, no longer sleeps, imprisons his wife and children in a room, and defends his private space by slashing the front door with a knife several times, as he has pinpointed the source of the name-calling and the insults to the outside corridor. It is these behavioural disorders and fear of his own violence that have prompted him to seek help.

He would refuse hospitalisation in the first instance as his wife was not given any warning, and as his family is dependent upon him (e.g., language barrier, literacy courses). He explains to me that he got them to come over a year ago. He talks about his wife and his three daughters (fourteen years old, eleven years old, and a baby of four months) with a great deal of warmth and emotion, and his difficulties in providing them with a decent standard of living, his anxieties in relation to the youngest (he has not known the older two since they were babies). He suggests to me that he would like to get things organised (by doing the weekly shop, leaving the neighbour to keep an eye out for them) and come back the following day to be hospitalised. He would return as promised; it is important to note that M.S. has always kept his word.

In terms of his biography, he is an only child. His father worked as a mason, but he *knew how to do everything*, particularly painting. After failing his high school-leaving certificate, M.S. gained an apprenticeship through his father as a carpenter, a trade he would practise for three years. M.S. says that he had been jealous of his father, who often carried out painting jobs, and that he had been drawn to the *colours*. It is during time spent at a construction site in Corsica, run by a family friend, that M.S. decides to stay in France. He settles in the Paris region, then twenty-two years old, and starts out as a painter and decorator.

Since then, he has continued to work within the same company, learning his craft on the job with professional painters. He returns to Morocco every year for his holidays and married in 1974. His wife lives on the same street as his parents. "She pierced my heart", he says, and insists that this is not an arranged marriage.

He had two daughters one after the other (the third was born in France). Each month he sends 1,000 francs (approximately €152, or, very roughly €760 in today's equivalent) to his wife and makes up his mind to bring her over to France once he has found a suitable apartment.

As for him, he lives in a hostel, the same one since he arrived in France, which is partly paid for by his employer. With a salary of a little less than €1,000 per month, he says that his lifestyle is adequate. In 1982, he finds an apartment, the rent of which he would go on paying for six years *for nothing*, preferring to stay in the hostel for companionship while he waits for his wife to go through the necessary administrative procedures in order to be able to join him in France.

Thus, very quickly, M.S. talks about his difficulties in supporting his family, his problems at work, and particularly his anxiety since his family's arrival. Gradually over the course of the interviews, he will make the connection between his delusional speech where "they tell him to get a divorce", where "they come between him and his wife", and his difficulties in his objective work situation, which progressively reaffirms this foreign "they" that persecutes him. These are difficulties that may be summed up by suffering as a result of the contradiction between:

1.   The psychic pressures connected to the organisation of work that necessitate virile defensive cooperation and recognition by the working collective, including outside the work situation on the one han.

2.   On the other, the psychic pressures underpinned by his family life: the recovery of individual desire in relation to his wife and daughters, putting him in a difficult position with the defensive ideology of virility between men, which had up to that point allowed him to cope with the psychic pressures of his work.

M.S. spoke at length about his work: "this trade, it's a bit of a love/hate relationship", he specifically emphasises the difference between indoor and outdoor worksites. Of outdoor sites he says:

> It's dangerous, there's the vertigo to contend with, the cold, it's slippery; but it's the others who give me courage. It's because there are four or five guys together. There is always one of us to be the first down. And if one is too scared, we shout up to him to come down. It's not work you can do alone.

He would often be the first to come down; he would make jokes, often he would give the orders. He was a valued team member, he was often entrusted with the position of site foreman if it was a small site or if the foreman was absent (Cru, 1983). He paid for the rounds. "There's a lot of banter that goes on at the bar", he says. It was these working conditions and specifically the relationship to risk that structured his life (space, time) outside of work. In this way, over the course of the interviews, he expressed to me:

1.   fear arising during renovation works, the constant confrontation with the risk of damage to corporal integrity, or even death

2.   anxiety that is at the root of challenging behaviours through which one might think that they are gaining control over the risk

3.   the functioning of *collective defence strategies*, the importance of mutual trust and group cohesion in order to be able to work (Dejours, 1980).

But M.S.'s working situation would gradually undergo changes, first in the very work organisation itself, bringing in its wake a breakdown of relationships of trust and cooperation between workers. For the past two years, the "boss's son" had been the one to take the reins of the family business. The boss himself had been a building site labourer and therefore knew the work (the practicalities of the task), and his employees, their practice, their skill set. "The son, he didn't know anything—he had done management studies", says M.S. He makes no distinction between his workers, calls for rates to be raised, places people regardless of skill (interior/exterior sites, etc.).

> Now, he's the boss. Previously we would liaise directly with the chief of works. When the young gun arrived, there were workers who he was tight with. These were the ones who were given the positions of responsibility. It's not the same anymore. Now there's the hotline, that is, for the squealers.

People are threatened and summoned to the office: so there are the "guys who talk"—a fundamental breach in this working collective and in the functioning of the defensive strategy. M.S. underscores the disappearance of the everyday conviviality, cohesion thus being undermined by the unidentified "squealers".

M.S. finds himself increasingly alone in the face of risk in his work. The arrival of his family during this same period and the birth of his third daughter exacerbate his psychological difficulties.

After some months of transition where he continued to see *his mates*, he bought himself a watch so he could get home "on time". His family and his personal desire were increasingly structuring his life outside work; no longer the group, which had already been shaken by a different organisation of work. He no longer shares his life with the other workers. *They* joke good-naturedly about him: "It's train-work-sleep".[1]

He is no longer able to take charge. His position is tenuous as he is no longer shored up by the defensive ideology of the trade. He must now face the danger alone (the fear of death, the anxiety in the face of his responsibilities to his family).

In this climate of progressive isolation, he sustains an accident at work that could have been fatal, followed by a psychic decompensation whereby, faced with a situation that is impossible to manage, *the hallucinations* tell him to get a divorce, thereby enabling him to rejoin the working collective.

As a coping strategy, he drinks; but this time alone.

The alternative, which becomes apparent during the course of the interviews, is a job with less risk, even if this would necessarily give rise to significant changes to his social and individual identity.

[Working] indoors is too hot, but at least it's clean. You don't get yourself all dirty. There's not so much paint splashing around as in redecorating. Outside it was too dangerous.

This history has therefore taken on meaning (it has been worked through, we would say in more technical terms) from the interpretation of the contradictions between the pressures of work and the affective investments of his private life, *in his current situation*. This work of interpretation is significantly different from that usually carried out in psychiatry, which takes no account of the context of the current social relationships of work; the only reference made being to the patient's diachrony and psychoneurotic history starting from his or her childhood past (Ludwig Binswanger, 1958). Indeed in practice, the retrocession of the psychotic disturbance was achieved without neuroleptic treatment. Mental stabilisation was accomplished by focusing exclusively on the patient's work situation, specifically through a change of job, the features of which were brought into focus by M.S. himself (interior worksites) during the course of psycho therapeutic treatment. It is unlikely that such a result would have been achieved without the reference point of the psychopathology of work.

Note

1. *métro-boulot-dodo*: this is metonymy referring to the everyday routine of an urban worker. It roughly connotes, "same old, same old".

References

Binswanger, L. (1958). *Le cas Suzanne Urban. Étude sur la schizophrénie*, Paris: Desclée de Brouwer.

Cru, D. (1983). «Les savoir-faire de prudence dans les métiers du bâtiment. Nouvelle contribution de la psychopathologie du travail à l'analyse des accidents et de la prévention dans le bâtiment». *Les cahiers médico-sociaux*, 27: 239–247.

Dejours, C. (1980). *Travail et usure mentale. Essai de psychopathologie du travail*. Paris: Le Centurion [fifth expanded edition, 2015].

CHAPTER THREE

"Doctor, can you get Alzheimer's at my age?" A mysterious deterioration of the cognitive functions in a forty-year-old patient

Marie-Pierre Guiho-Bailly and Patrick Lafond

I n day-to-day clinical practice, attention to the professional lives of patients—to the role played by work in their lives, their mental functioning, the deterioration of their health or their recovery—is not a given for psychiatric care providers.

Within the framework of psychiatric care, the patient's occupation is most often referred to from the point of view of occupational therapy, "capacity" for work, or his or her occupational rehabilitation in terms of therapeutic activity or psycho-social rehabilitation plans; decisions to be taken in terms of sick-leave or disability classification; or social support as part of a process of recognition of disabled worker *status* or the search for employment in an "ordinary" or "protected" environment when the person's mental state is considered sufficiently stabilised to support professional activity.

These are the features of psychiatric pathology, of personality disorders, of scalable modalities of illness, which—downstream of the care plan—guide the clinicians' considerations over the relation to work, which is considered primarily in terms of autonomy and social integration.

The absence of job-related issues in a patient who consults for temporary psychic decompensation, and whose state of health does not appear to necessitate sick-leave, may even result in any questioning about work being disregarded completely.

Too often we find medical records in which concrete specifics of the profession practiced, professional career history, or the particular features of the subjective relation to work and its progression, are entirely omitted, apart from only scant mention of the current profession, in a one-word note on the patient record sheet. And yet, when we look further into this item on the sheet . . .

Most frequently—outside of the specific situations where, from the outset, mental suffering is directly attributed to the work situation by the person involved—patients themselves will participate in this process of concealment, considering that their professional lives "don't concern" the clinician, other than to assess the temporary impact of their state of health on their fitness for work.

The majority of the time, in truth, what is at issue for the patient dovetails with that of the consulting practitioner: to specify the signs and symptoms (semiology) of the emotional disturbance, to establish a diagnosis, to formulate aetiological hypotheses by first eliminating the psychiatric expression of a somatic problem, then to investigate the elements of personal and family history and the structural modalities of mental functioning, which may shed light on the clinical presentation and guide the therapeutic applications.

History

It was within this classic view of psychiatric clinical practice that we provided consultation to Jeannine, a forty-year-old woman, married with two children, whose case was already known to us as we had monitored her progress for some time, three years previously, following a suicide attempt.[1]

During this initial patient management, Jeannine had spoken about her suicidal act (a massive ingestion of prescription drugs) as a questioning of the meaning of her life: to give a warning or to disappear? Her intentions remain poorly established, but Jeannine knows that she can no longer continue to live without questioning the meaning of her existence, her priorities, her "usefulness", her identity as a woman.

Much attention is paid to the circumstances of the women in her family: her eldest daughter who has recently left home to start her own life; her mother who is ageing; how she herself has thus far thrown herself into her role as a daughter, mother, wife, housekeeper, who is proud of her "gifts", she says, which make her an excellent cook, a skilled seamstress, much-admired for her flair in home decorating, the beauty of her garden, for her creativity, her handiness, and constant innovation.

There is no self-devaluation in her remarks, no attacks on her self-worth, no doubts as to her skills nor the love of her family. There is however an anxious apprehension towards, and a pejorative vision of, the future, of the return of family life to life as a couple, to ageing, illness, and death.

Her children are grown up and are beginning to fly the nest, everything is "completed" at home, and her husband does not see where the problem is—How to deal with the time they have left to live? What meaning will her life now take on? Why "go on", and for whom?

For some time now, Jeannine had been formulating the plan to seek "a bit of" work, but finds nothing suitable in a lean job market. Furthermore, her existential questioning and the temptation of suicide spark reminiscences relating to her childhood history, her family history, raising a question mark over her affective and sexual life, and Jeannine begins psychotherapy.

Her capacity for mentalization and verbalisation is good, her idea associations are fecund, with a wealth of preconscious functioning, dreams, and enlightening connections between personal history and current subjective experience.

Little by little, her plan to take up an occupation establishes itself and becomes clear; in keeping with the socially valued "feminine qualities" that have underpinned her identity in domestic and family work, Jeannine, increasingly determinedly, seeks employment in the "fabrics line": clothing, decoration, dressmaking, sales. Finally, she finds a sales assistant position in a recently-established department store specialising in clothing and upholstery.

In her chosen profession, full-time as she wanted, a permanent contract from the start, minimal distance between home and workplace, everything appears to be the best possible outcome in Jeannine's career plan. Furthermore, with regained psycho-emotional balance, she puts an end to a psychotherapy she no longer feels the need for.

Decompensation

A year has passed when Jeannine comes back for a consultation. She comes across as defeated, emaciated, worn out, almost haggard. She says she is exhausted, irritable, suffering from insomnia and slowed ideo-motor activity. But the symptoms she finds most worrying of all are the appearance and the progressive worsening of cognitive and psychomotor disturbances over the past few months.

From the outset, Jeannine reveals that she does not recognise any of the symptoms whatsoever in her current state from her previous decompensation; this is an entirely different state . . . "Doctor, can a person my age get Alzheimer's?"

Jeannine is losing her memory: she no longer knows where she puts her things, leaves tasks half-finished, and has already forgotten where she is going before she arrives. Going from one activity to another without even realising it, she finds here and there at home traces of tasks begun but not completed, without being able to remember the moment of, nor the reason for, the interruption.

She has serious attention and concentration disturbances. She no longer has any memory retention for what people tell her, no longer able to follow a conversation, "always one question behind in my replies", and she struggles to gather her ideas in order to formulate an appropriate response. Like her thoughts, her words no longer come readily to her. Her thoughts flit from one to the other, and then disappear in turn. She can no longer follow a film or television programme: she loses the thread of the plot, her attention can be distracted at any time, for no real reason. She can no longer read, as she forgets the contents of the previous page almost as soon as she has read it, despite her interest in the book.

But there is worse from her point of view: she is no longer "good with her hands". A person who is so proud of her manual dexterity and creative abilities is now losing her skills and becoming increasingly clumsy. Everything slips from her grasp; she breaks one object after another; she messes up all her recipes, even the simplest and the ones she does most often; she can no longer do the things she has done a thousand times over, as if all of this accumulated knowledge, which had become an everyday reflex action, a source of pleasure and pride, had been deconstructed.

What she still manages to do now takes her infinitely longer and never gives her any satisfaction, with a rough imperfect quality that no longer meets the standard of being "fit to be seen". It is as if she were losing all her faculties. As if she had early-onset dementia.

All of these symptoms terrify her. She dare not touch anything, takes refuge in her bed as soon as she can, dreads occasions like family and social reunions, and begins to fear for her job since, she says, "these symptoms are starting to flare up at work too", from forgetfulness to clumsiness.

With this loss of skill and adroitness which she experiences in her intelligence and in her body, Jeannine feels "more elderly than mad", more "unwell" than depressed or anxious. Her major fear: suffering from a cerebral pathology, from "early-onset senility".

Faced with this clinical picture, a full somatic examination is effectively ordered, in order to eliminate an organic cerebral disorder, whether metabolic, infectious, neurovascular, tumourous, neuro-degenerative. Every test comes back negative. Somatically, she is given a clean bill of health.

So . . . is it mental . . .?

In terms of psychodynamic approach, we come back to the patient's recent life events (losses, departures, and changes), her emotional life and her subjective relation to ageing, to illness, to death—topics we had addressed two years ago.

Unlike the previous period of treatment, there is no intelligible connection and the symptoms persist.

Unsuccessful in this process of verbal psychotherapy, with a "trial" antidepressant treatment also proving ineffective and, in truth, perplexed by this psychic pain and this clinical picture, we offer Jeannine a different approach, combining:

1. On the one hand, interviews with the psychiatrist, for now focusing on the present, the tangible; on the actuality.

2. On the other hand, a psycho-corporal approach using relaxation techniques, to be carried out by another therapist, a nurse specialised in this treatment technique, with the aim of better understanding the connections between psychic and bodily experience, and helping Jeannine to re-appropriate this body that she no longer has any control over, and of which she says she

fears "will give out on her" at any time, in dramatic fashion, particularly at her workplace.

During relaxation therapy, Jeannine displays the disturbances by which she is afflicted. In his notes, the therapist records the following observations:

> Mrs B pays particular attention to the sensation of being rushed, of fear of being unable to manage her time; of being unable to finish or in fact unable to perform faster or too fast, a sensation felt both in her professional as well as family life.

Her relation to time, to rhythms, to stages, and to deadlines will be central to Jeannine's relaxation therapy:

> She takes in a part of the conclusion when her mind flits to something else. Distracted, she does not take in the rest of the conclusion and she worries that she has missed some of the steps. She realises that this is how she operates, including at her work. Today, for example, she fixates on the announcement that the next meeting is in a month's time.

At the conclusion of the relaxation therapy, the therapist points out that, in every session, Jeannine continues to make the connection with her experience at work, whereas she has never mentioned her earlier experience nor her previous psychic decompensation.

"Like at work", in the relaxation sessions Jeannine is unable to follow her train of thought, or to see her plans through to completion, step by step. Her thoughts are dispersed, fleeting; what she intends to do fades away; she is no longer sure of what she has actually done or what remains for her to do.

Jeannine takes cognisance of the fact that this phenomenon is accentuated, even produced, by two different types of "interference" (*parasitage*):

1. Hypersensitivity to external stimuli, here mainly auditory: "She says that it is impossible for her to concentrate whatever the task may be, that the slightest stimuli immediately distract her."

2. Obsessive thinking about tasks carried out or to be carried out: "Her mind wanders, recalling the activities of the day before or anticipating the tasks ahead."

Her inability to relax, as to concentrate, is associated with a snagging of her mental functioning at perception-awareness level, leading to hyper vigilance to external stimuli, and to failure of the preconscious with a repression of fantasmatic life: "Mrs B explains that she has no images because she is unable to manage to concentrate; her mind wanders, but without content, without representation." Her only escape mechanism is somnolence or lower levels of vigilance. But her "inability to let the images come" upsets Jeannine, who is well aware of the contrast with her "normal" psychic functioning.

Work situation

Parallel to this, in the psychiatrist's interviews, Jeannine alludes to how her work situation has changed since her initial hiring over a year ago, in an organisational environment where the margins of autonomy were experienced as adequate, with a line manager she described as "understanding"; her responsibility for one department was shared with a colleague working part-time and with whom she was free to negotiate how they organised their working hours, as long as between them they covered the customer helpdesk in this store open to the public for fifty-two hours a week.

The situation has since changed, with the arrival of a new manager responsible for rolling out restructuring operations passed by national general management with the aim of better management of human resources by making adjustments to day-to-day adaptability and timetable flexibility. This they do by increasing the range of duties of each of the sales staff, who are considered to be interchangeable and now suddenly responsible for ensuring customer service, the management of stock, order placing, handling the pieces of cloth or the clothing racks and boxes, but also to act as replacement at short notice for an absent or unavailable colleague in different departments, to instruct new recruits, all of whom are on a fixed-term contract.

As Jeannine explains, it is becoming much more difficult to think ahead, to organise her time, which is already subject to the irregularities of customer flow. She has to be everywhere at once, often unpredictably. Her working hours also become irregular, at times changing from one day to the next.

But the most painful of all for Jeannine to bear is the loss of autonomy and the lack of recognition in a job that is now controlled at all times by a micromanager who denies her skills and experience, who constantly intervenes to give the order to interrupt her current task, and to immediately devote herself to another task that is judged to be a priority and that needs to be done yesterday.

The atmosphere among the staff has deteriorated. Spontaneously helping-out another colleague has disappeared, swept away by instructions for additional support on an ad hoc basis, which is always experienced as an unfairly imposed overloading of work, where previously, "lending a hand" as soon as one's own task was completed never posed any problem.

Solidarity is difficult to build with the new recruits, who are perceived as submissive and "silent" as a result of their precarious status, which Jeannine can well understand but it hits her hard, with an overwhelming sense of loneliness, given that, furthermore, the old girls are disappearing one by one, either temporarily or permanently: leave taken for a gastric ulcer for one, depression for another, an unplanned but welcome pregnancy to get out of work, resignation, and so on.

Gradually, Jeannine realises that "if she is functioning like this, including at work" this is not because some cognitive disorder of indeterminate origin is impacting upon her capacity for work, but rather because her work's new organisational modalities are dismantling her cognitive skills, now outside of work too. Jeannine has been "sabotaged".

For their part, the therapists, pooling their observations, also validate this hypothesis: the cognitive and psychomotor disturbances presented by Jeannine are not the cause of the difficulties she encounters in her work, but rather they are the consequence of her work.

The ad hoc flexibility, the obsession with deadlines, the incessant interruption of her task with orders that must be carried out immediately (the "auditory stimuli" that she is as much apprehensive of as listening out for, in a permanent state of alert). These render impossible any "follow-up" of her work as much as any completion of her ongoing psychomotor programming, and they strip Jeannine not only of her autonomy of action but also of her autonomy of thought.

The chain still broken from the now-prohibited initiative-taking, she scrambles, increasingly clumsily, from order to counter-order, from irregular customer flow and the unpredictability of the tasks to be assigned her, which are always unfinished, but always present in her mind, saturating her field of consciousness with their incompletion.

Jeannine is no longer satisfied with, and even less proud of, this fragmented work, which is neither completed nor pending, of which she can no longer see the end, of which she no longer has a view of the bigger picture. This is work that, for her, has become unrepresentable and that is scarcely any longer presentable for the evaluation of others.

Her coming to awareness of the connections between her current mental state and the characteristics of the work organisation leads to a rapid decrease in Jeannine's anxiety and sleep disturbance. Jeannine is then able to speculate upon the nature of her symptoms, at the point where she realises that other employees have reacted differently (gastric ulcer, depression, etc.) to a work situation that was, in appearance, identical for all. She takes stock of her personal need for being in control, of her difficulty in not keeping her hand in what she begins or undertakes, in accepting that people will interfere or that people go about things differently to her.

A particularly striking relaxation session, as much for her therapist as for her, is one in which Jeannine experiences the relaxation of her head and neck as a totally new sensation; one she describes as a "discovery", the session experienced as a "freeing-up".

Jeannine eventually accepts leave, which she had refused up to that point for fear of losing her job, but a minor and planned surgical procedure enables her to legitimise it. Over the course of this three-month leave, all her symptoms would gradually disappear.

This observation leads Jeannine to question and to raise the issue of occupational health: the occupational physician, who was contacted with Jeannine's permission, confirms "the epidemic" among the company's staff and informs us of the warning already given in this connection; Jeannine communicates with other colleagues, writes a letter to general management co-signed with another colleague, also on leave, then begins proceedings with the Labour Inspectorate. Her commitment to this action aids in her psychic restructuring, through her regained pleasure in "functioning" healthily.

The resumption of work first occurs halfway through her treatment, later Jeannine would negotiate part-time hours for personal reasons—"to give time for the dust to settle"—before opting for a year's extended leave, with the idea of planning for a career change if there have been no developments in the situation at the company.

The occupational physician documented his report and clearly announced to management his intention to carry out regular monitoring, over time, of the reported risk to employee health.

Subsequently, changes would take place in the organisational chart and in the organisation of work, with a change in direct line manager and the reintroduction of margins of autonomy for employees in the collective management of work, improvements deemed sufficient for Jeannine to finally venture back to her position in the company, with no recurrence of her symptoms and with the possibility of terminating her psychiatric care.

* * *

In psychiatry, the patients' work in actual fact remains unknown; the role of work in mental life and the subjective relation to work remain unexplored.

Despite the clues that punctuated Jeannine's speech, it would be weeks—if not months—before we were able to understand what she was saying about her work, which was at once both a sublimatory channel and source of suffering.

It took coming up against an unsuccessful comprehensive approach that originally focused exclusively upon the psycho-familial dimension, on her emotional life, before venturing to address the psychosocial dimension of her mental life, until the line of our clinical investigation switched focus and our listening became oriented towards the—here central—place of work in the genesis of her present-day emotional disturbance.

Note

1. An initial presentation of this clinical history took place on 6 December 1996 as part of a joint communication with Ghislaine Doniol-Shaw, LATTS-CNRS ergonomist, at the European Meetings organised by the research group, GDR MAGE (*Marché du travail et genre*, labour market and gender), on the subject "Health and work; service sector jobs" (G. Doniol-Shaw, & M.-P. Guiho-Bailly, "Emploi, conditions de travail et santé des employées dans les services", *Les cahiers du Mage*, 4/96, 15–33).

CHAPTER FOUR

"Centrality of work" and sexuality theory

Christophe Dejours

C ontrary to what is generally accepted, work is not simply a backdrop against which the plot and intrigue of psycho-neurosis is played out. At least this is the point of view we shall seek to argue by focusing on the psychodynamics of work. The clinical data amassed by this discipline since the post-war period indeed suggests that work occupies a central role in character development, from early childhood to maturity. We will not consider here the impact of work on psychic development before adolescence. Instead we shall confine ourselves to discussing the role occupied by social relations of work in the construction of sexual identity, and to analysing the difficulties these give rise to, up to and including in the *erotic economy* itself, during adolescence. While the aim of this chapter is conceptual, it is beyond the present scope to enter into a full discussion of the theoretical dimension. Indeed, our primary aim is to gather together the clinical elements required by us to address the question of the *analytic listening* to, and the interpretation of, the dimension of work in psychic functioning. As such we shall draw on the psychotherapeutic work that took place with a young woman in her late adolescence.

From the patient's initial request to the psychoanalytic
construction of a neurotic problem complex that was sexual
in nature

The patient had just turned twenty when she came to my consulting room for the first time. She had made a request for psychotherapy—in order to analyse her behaviour, she says! Why? Because for several years she has suffered from abdomino-pelvic pain and she was wondering whether this might have something to do with what was going on inside her head.

Miss Mulvir is slim and well-proportioned. She has a face that is a little out of the ordinary and which suggests that, when she is older, she might bear a certain resemblance to some of Toulouse-Lautrec's portraits. Her chin is strong and prominent. Her straight nose descends interminably, as if it were trying to join her chin. She dresses with a great deal of care and stylish detail.

Consequently, she would alternate between elegant and stylish outfits—stretch jeans, pointed high-heeled boots, sometimes leather jackets. Her silhouette is long and supple, her wrists and ankles are very slender, her psychomotor pattern is feminine and without affectation.

She lives with her parents. Her relationship with them is marked by incessant fighting, sometimes very badly, in particular with her mother who seems to wear the trousers at home. Her mother is irritable, especially since she has begun to encounter difficulties in her professional career. She had to leave the company she worked for and has gone through a period of unemployment. She found another job—it was less skilled than her previous one, but she was obliged to accept it, as nothing better was on offer. In her work as a secretary, she constantly complains about the misogyny that reigns in her work environment. The patient's father is a "technical sales representative". Some time previously, he had suffered from a gastric ulcer and had considered psychotherapy, but did not go through with the idea. He, however, encouraged his daughter to take the necessary steps towards therapy.

The situation relaxed significantly in this small family unit when Miss Mulvir reached the age of eighteen. Her parents then considered her free to do whatever she liked, and that they were no longer responsible for her. She chose to remain under the parental roof, after having negotiated some minimum requirements of shared living.

Miss Mulvir has a sister two years her senior, who had left the family home, and who lived with a boy under particularly difficult relational circumstances. This man was alcoholic, often violent, and unfaithful. He finally revealed that he was bisexual. Since the breakup, her sister has cloistered herself away, living a very withdrawn and solitary existence, as if she were no longer able to muster any appetite for life or experience any joy. Miss Mulvir is very concerned by what has become of her sister. She makes repeated efforts to get her out of the house, to cheer her up and try to patch up the relationship with her parents. Indeed, she describes these things as if the fate of her sister were one of her fundamental concerns, as if her sister's problems might be harmful to her own future.

Miss Mulvir works. Here, also, she encounters difficulties. Relationships with her male colleagues are experienced as a kind of rivalry, particularly with her boss, which works to her disadvantage. She notices that when conflict with her boss worsens she feels an intense rage building up in her, which she would repress—with the result that she experiences acute abdominal pain. These stomachaches are extremely painful, and occur whenever she feels frustrated or anxious. When she sat her *baccalauréat* examinations, for example, she could only take part in the exams for one hour out of every four— the other three were spent in the toilet, doubled up in pain. These were neither experienced as spasms, nor a really upset stomach, but rather an inner stabbing sensation.

I am taken aback by the very direct way in which she talks about her outbursts of anger, during which she is subject to feelings of wanting to lash out violently at anyone in the vicinity. At the same time, she appears so physically frail and feminine that it was difficult to see her being transformed into a brute, less still how she would be able to exert any violence whatsoever against anyone. At other times, she might also talk about her fear of men and violence, as well as of all the manifestations of a power struggle based on physical strength.

To my questions about possible forms of violence practiced in her family, she replies that these are extremely rare. Then again, her mother would sometimes give in to truly fearsome fits of rage and screaming. From this, she has retained a sensitivity that verges on genuine panic as soon as someone raises their voice. This will give rise to another attack of stomach pains. As for her father, he is rarely violent. On occasion, he has given her a couple of slaps, but she thinks that this is the right way of going about things, and that it is better to have been actively corrected rather than to have been too spoiled, which would have led (as she notes in some of her acquaintances who had the misfortune of having an upbringing that was too lax) to her becoming a wretched soul who finds life difficult. She points out, however, that when her father was really angry he would give her, and her sister, a couple of good kicks on the backside. At this, she smiles.

In her second session, she wanted to explain something she had previously forgotten to tell me, and which could be significant. The other day she had been watching a television programme about dreams. That made her think of the dreams that she often had as a child. She would "imagine" that she had a brother—an older brother, who possessed every quality imaginable: he was physically strong and intelligent, he knew a lot about many things, he was knowledge-able also with regard to all the problems that people are unsure about in their everyday life, and he was emotionally and mentally very stable. "A superman," she added, just in case I had not understood. She smiled upon recalling her dreams.

She would return on several occasions to this mythical brother she had dreamt up. She says that this brother: "had a strong desire to . . ." and stops herself mid-sentence: "No! I would have liked to be this brother, and in my dreams it often happened that I became this brother." She saw herself in the school playground, the courtyard planted with trees . . . and she was endowed with a formidable phys-ical strength allowing her to climb the trees and to even fly clear over them. With this new-found force, she would also have been able to put it to use whenever she wanted to give anyone around her a good thumping.

She told her parents about her dreams, after the programme had finished. They were dumbstruck. Her mother then told her that, in fact, she did have a brother, who would have been around thirty now. He and she would have had the exact same age difference as in Miss Mulvir's dream if he had not died at birth. Could she have had any knowledge of this, given that her parents, for their part, had, until then, never mentioned the existence of this brother, neither to her nor her sister?

In her dreams she had given a name to this brother, one phoneti-cally similar to that of her father.

This problem complex concerning identification with men is also a feature of her professional relationships and her investments outside of her work environment: for example, she had decided to take a course in muscle-development—not body-building, as she was careful to point out. That gave her some degree of physical strength as well as self-confidence. And yet, she knows that there is no sense in imagining that one day she will be as strong as a man or that she will have the muscle power to fight or to compete with a man. But she is very pleased whenever someone asks her to loosen a bolt or unscrew a lid on a jar, for example.

As we see from her second session, her free associations lead her to speculate upon her sexual identity. She is not, she states, attracted to women in any way. She does not feel that she is homosexual. Quite the contrary, she prefers the company of men. In her remarks, I notice that she repeatedly uses the expression: "a stab in the back" or "a blow from behind". She thinks that women can attack from behind, that they are backstabbers. But not men! She would never expect such behaviour from them. And yet, at her workplace, the colleague she had problems with has stabbed her in the back. She works in an environment that is, traditionally, exclusively male. This colleague, who is also her boss, a man of around fifty years old, does not take kindly to the presence of Miss Mulvir, with her feminine and fashionable attire, who does the same work as he does, at times probably with more care, more diligence, and more skill than he. So he "stabs her in the back", by talking about her in a very derogatory way to management. His attacks from behind come as such a shock to her that she ends up wondering if these colleagues are men at all. When she has something to say to someone, she darn well says it to their face!

This is quite clearly a complex problem of a psychosexual nature. But how are these issues expressed in the erotic register?

Miss Mulvir liked to go out a lot; every Saturday evening she would go to one or other of the nightclubs in the surrounding area. She would dance, chat up guys, and go to bed with a new one each time. On each occasion, however, she was disappointed. Sexual intercourse was painful for her. Her vaginal secretions were insufficient and penetration often led to vaginal bleeding, with the mucous membrane being torn. She never felt that she was in love—or at most the feeling was extremely short-lived. That being the case she would build far-fetched plans for the future, which had nothing to do with the actual state of the situation in which she found herself. Built up entirely on rational calculations, her planning left almost no room for fantasy or romance.

Her psychotherapy has now gone on for two years. The conflict with her parents has become acute. Her mother is now retired. Her father, in turn, is soon to retire and the atmosphere at home is deteriorating. Her mother is unbearable and cantankerous. Miss Mulvir wants to leave and find her own place, but both her parents, who in all likelihood fear finding themselves alone faced with each other, are opposed to this plan. Despite this, she manages to leave and settles into an H.L.M. (*Habitation a loyer modéré*, equivalent to council housing). One day, she reacts furiously to her parents' attitude. They cannot understand what has got into her. Unconvincingly, they attempt to justify themselves in the wake of the reproaches she makes against them. Exasperated, they end up declaring that all this is undoubtedly the result of that "bullshit psychoanalysis" that has turned her against them. They refuse to answer her insistent questions about her childhood, about their own pasts, and so on. As increasingly often they goad her about this "idiot analyst", and as the situation seems to have reached an impasse, I suggest to her that, if she is in agreement, she may reply to them that "if they are so interested in the analyst, they can make an appointment with him".

This takes place without further ado.

After this meeting, the conflict with her parents de-escalates dramatically. Now free of guilt, her parents agree to answer all of Miss Mulvir's questions, which allows a release from the silences and enables her to put an end to the interpretations that tended towards the persecutory in this patient. Until this point, Miss Mulvir had only encountered, in the course of her Saturday-night outings, psychopaths and perverts; "tattooed guys" who were ready with their fists and who were often alcoholic. Beginning with this step, her sexuality changes orientation and she begins to meet men who are "less hard".

In spite of what she had said at the very beginning, sometimes she did dream of being with a woman partner, especially when she masturbated. She asked me, in a very sincere and truly puzzled way, whether, deep down, she was homosexual or not.

If we restrict ourselves to analysing the connection between her sexual disappointments and the identificatory dynamic of her relationship with her parents, the situation seems clear enough. She refuses to identify with her mother, and she takes upon her shoulders her father's life-project. When he began working, he was a technician—she was too. He managed to advance his career to become a technical salesman—and that was her dream too at that point. Although her identification with her father is clear enough, it was not accompanied by any *idealisation* of him. Quite the contrary: Miss Mulvir felt that her parents' lifestyle was deplorable—their conjugal fidelity, their weekly sexual relations followed by her mother's ritual bathroom routine, and so on.

Resistance to analysis or struggle against acquiescence? The irreducibility of the social to the sexual sphere

And yet, the work of psychotherapy comes almost to a standstill. The absence of regression, the absence of hostility towards the analyst, and the absence of repetition of childhood conflicts in transference: all of these empty any interpretation of all mutative effectiveness. It seems to me that this is a typical situation, but while everything appears to be in place for reappropriation followed by freeing up in the patient, nothing is moving. We cannot cite a negative therapeutic reaction, nor a failure syndrome; her parents' responsiveness makes it impossible to support the hypothesis of a subclinical symbiotic relationship.

It was only by displacing the centre of gravity of the analytical focus that new perspectives were opened up. Miss Mulvir did not manage to find in her mother an identificatory reference point, but this was not because her mother had not been sufficiently loving. It had more to do with the fact that the patient steadfastly refused to give in to certain expectations and to resign herself to the kind of being-in-the-world as woman that her mother exemplified: a faithful woman, with no panache, a secretary-typist unhappy in her work, aggressive towards her husband and her children, frustrated in her social life, and disappointed by the fact that her retirement would offer no prospect of emancipation. This woman-being holds no attraction for the patient, whichever way she looked at it, particularly on a professional and social level.

As for Miss Mulvir, she had real "ambitions" for her career. Admittedly, these ambitions did not resemble those that society likes to praise, which are generally borrowed from the world of the moneyed classes. She had sat her *baccalauréat* exams in technical subjects—a difficult course—and had gone on to do an advanced vocational training certificate (BTS). She was working in an electronics workshop, where she did prototype assembly, often in a "clean room" environment. She had by then progressed to being an electronics technician in the "thick-layer" department. She had always been good at maths. She wanted to continue in that field, then move on to a technical sales role. But in her own family, social, financial, and work situation, these plans seemed to be incompatible with a particular social model of women. In fact, around her, in an environment of workers, employees, and technicians, she was the only woman. These men's girlfriends were "kept women", miserable creatures who had renounced any social ambition to have nothing more to hope for but motherhood, domesticity, and unskilled employment, while the men were chauvinistic, coarse, unaffectionate, and were only after one thing from women: "the notch in the bedpost".

Now, in the course of her relations with boys, a consequence of what she calls her "sexual need" and her inability to tolerate sexual abstinence—in spite of the unpleasant after-effects and her lack of erotic pleasure—she essentially encounters partners who embody everything that she detests: machismo, affective indifference, a tendency to drink too much, and to be rude and uncouth.

With these men, she seemed to be seeking *the recognition of an identity* on an *equal footing*. She feels no affection for these men—they were merely one-night stands. She is not interested in them, and she is not looking to make any concessions. These encounters are strictly self-centred. Above all, she wanted these men—particularly the most chauvinistic of them—to show her consideration and respect. It sometimes happened that the situation was less cut-and-dried: the relationship was reversed, and she is the one who becomes contemptuous whenever she speaks of them.

What she is seeking, unconsciously, is to be endowed with "social standing" by chauvinistic men, to then be able to establish with them an erotic relationship that took into account the reciprocal otherness between the sexes. But this would be a relationship based on equality, and not on a system of dominating *vs.* dominated. From the point of view of this quest for her sexual identity, this is a conflict that turned sour, because the predominance of the social relations of domination and her struggle against them almost always leads her to behave like a man, which does not in the least allow her to assert her identity as a woman. In this kind of social environment, in fact, no woman can ever be the equal of a man. She should accept the fact that she is destined to be dominated. But Miss Mulvir wants both to have a relationship in which there is *differentiation* between the sexual roles, and a relationship of *equality* divested of these relationships of domination. Is this an impossible wish?

At this point, the analyst often commits an error. He or she will assume, in the case of women, that their position as a woman and their acceptance of domination by men, in social relations, work, and sexuality, are roughly identical. Their refusal of domination on the one hand, and their refusal to submit to the renunciation of self-fulfilment in the social and professional fields on the other, are then understood as a phallic claim, or wish for a penis, and not as a desire for the construction and recognition of an emancipated female sexual identity.

We are now at the heart of sexuality theory and its connections with work. To analyse the conflict between expectations in relation to the construction of identity in the field of *work*, and the expectation in relation to the construction of identity in the *erotic* field, we need to break with conventional conceptualisations of the relationships between work and psychic functioning.

Traditionally, work as such does not form part of the psychoanalytic investigative or conceptual field. However, when it is accorded a place in psychoneurotic problem complexes, it is, generally speaking, with regard to men or male adolescents. This is the case in Freud's conceptualisations on sublimation (Freud, 1910c). As far as we may sum up what the literature in general psychopathology advances, we may educe two typical sets of problems:

1. The professional choice, the enactment of issues relating to social investments, sublimation, identifications, idealisations, and the forms of expression of the failures of these in the adolescent or adult (unconscious vectorisation towards work).

2. The implications of the work situation on the psychic and affective life of the adult, or if not more generally, on mental or somatic health (social vectorisation towards the subject).

In these two problem complexes, we implicitly accept the idea that work constitutes a dimension that is ontologically *external* to the subject, a *reality element* into which the elements relating to the functioning of society (hierarchy, economic dimension, etc.) and the materiality of the pressures connected with professional activity (gestures, skills, know-how, knowledge that must be acquired and put into practice, expertise, performance, etc.) become condensed.

While this reality may be unsettling or traumatic, it is merely considered by psychoanalysis to be radically foreign, posing only a problem of articulation to subjective life, one that is generally considered in terms of psychic adaptation or adjustment.

In this context, and when it is a source of suffering, the subjective relation to work is approached from two angles, between which each author chooses on the basis of his or her presuppositions.

Or society is considered, on the whole, to be endowed with immense power, incomparably greater than that of unconscious desire, thereby establishing a balance of power similar to that between an evil and selfish giant on the one side, and a defenceless and helpless child on the other. We then readily speak in terms of stress or aggressology, of adaptation or maladaption (Cherniss, 1980).

Alternatively we consider that society is what it is and that it is the same for everyone. Psychoneurotic disorders, even if they were to take the staging of the relation to work as a privileged area of expression, would not call into question the contingency of work in their aetiology. Indeed, the potentially deleterious impact of work would not depend on society but upon individual psychoneurotic fragilities, inherited from infantile neurosis. One then speaks in terms of trauma theory.

These approaches all have relevance, even if they do not serve to tell us whether it is the subject or society that is responsible for the suffering and the sickness of the subject who works (or who does not work).

From theoretical references in sociology to the formation of work-focused psychoanalytic listening

And so, in the following paragraphs, I shall offer up a further step towards the analysis of the subjective relation to work, by following three directions:

1. Listening specifically to the intermeshing between the *erotic* and the *desexualised* in symptom formation and the working through of transference.

2. Elaborating this intermeshing at the most crucial time, namely that of adolescence.

3. Finally, reflecting upon praxic content, starting from the clinical phenomenology of women, because it is here, in my view, that the difficulties are compounded for psychoanalytic listening. Our conception of work is forged from sexist presuppositions. When listening to women, psychoanalysts find it difficult to evaluate the significance of the relationships of domination of men over women in the sphere of work.

Miss Mulvir thus clearly formulates, from the very beginning of her psychotherapy, the desire to make a career doing what she enjoys and what she has chosen to do, to win her material independence, her freedom, by her own merits, that is to say, her social emancipation vis-à-vis the relationships of domination of men over women, and last but not least, to escape the fate that befell her mother. In sum, she wants both to have a promising professional career—or move up the social ladder—*and* to be a woman.

However, both her *professional* environment and her *social* milieu are an obstacle to this, her only remaining prospects being to give up the whole idea, accept disappointment, and see her future as dreary. Put another way, what was offered to Miss Mulvir by social and professional constraints was the choice between being-as-woman and self-fulfilment in the social sphere. This is a typical situation, one that differs markedly from the one that is presented to men. For the latter, it is clear that self-fulfilment in the erotic-emotional sphere goes hand-in-hand with self-fulfilment in the professional and social fields—indeed, the one reinforces the other.

Accordingly it seems to be the norm, in a couple, for the woman to accept the renunciation of her self-fulfilment in the social sphere (i.e., a career or a profession), to leave the field open for the man's self-fulfilment. Likewise, it seems to be the norm that she should accept unskilled and subsistence labour so that the man can finish his studies; that she should give up her career to take care of the domestic work or be available for the various incidents and mishaps that crop up in family life with children; and finally that she should accept financial dependence upon the man. He, on the other hand, gains ever more autonomy and power within the dynamics of these relationships in the private sphere.

Undoubtedly, more equitable configurations between men and women are possible. There are couples who strive to respect each other's autonomy, equal rights, and social and professional aspirations, and who succeed, at the same time, in acknowledging the differences in sexual identity between the two partners. It may even be that in such a way the most favourable conditions are met for the construction of sexual identities, insofar as love relationships would then be divested of any reference to the social domination of men over women. But perfect equality remains the exception and reducing inequality, in the same way as reducing the use of relationships of domination by men, remain a minority in contemporary society.

With regard to Miss Mulvir, in any case, her social and professional world remains fairly hermetic to this progression. For Miss Mulvir, the price to pay for this stubbornness in asserting her career choices results in an impasse in her erotic and emotional life. In her world, it seems that there is *no woman* apt to constitute a *model* of the emancipation *and* the sexual success that she dreams of.

A dozen or so years prior to the start of this psychotherapy, I had been engaged in research on the psychodynamics and psychopathology of work. It was, however, only two years into therapy that I personally managed, under the guidance of sociology researchers, to understand the concept of "social relationships of sex" and the indissociable connection between, on the one hand, social relationships of sex and *social relationships of work*; and between social relationships of work and *relationships of domination*, or relationships of production and relationships of reproduction, on the other (Kergoat, 1982, 1984).

The case presentation outlined above draws from the work of Danièle Kergoat and Helena Hirata on the analysis of conflicts between the attainment of sexual identity in the erotic field and the attainment of identity in the professional (and social) field (Hirata & Kergoat, 1988). During these first two years of psychotherapy, my listening focus, which was open to the problem complex of work, however remained largely focused on the repetition of infantile neurosis and on the psychopathological susceptibility to the psychosomatic (abdomino-pelvic pains, frigidity, musculo-tendonal pathology brought on by dancing, to which Miss Mulvir also devoted herself, and which there is not the scope here to discuss).

For me, the assimilation of the sociological concepts of the social relationships of sex and of the social and sexual division of labour was followed by a true existential paradigm shift. This was the price to pay for Miss Mulvir's words suddenly awakening other echoes within me. Until that point, her sexual psychopathology had appeared to me as relating to the wish for a penis and to a fairly typical refusal of castration, but now it could be understood as the ill-fated struggle against something that, in a social construct, was able to function as a socio-professional barrier to her aspirations, as a social obstacle to her ambition to be a woman *and* to be looked upon as *equal to men*—which is not at all the same thing as *being* a man. The patient's quest could be seen as a struggle against *muliebrity*. "Muliebrity" is the status conferred upon women by the *social relationships of sex*. It is a more-or-less stereotyped social construct—Miss Mulvir's mother, on the whole, is a typical example of this within her own milieu. The patient's wanting-to-be-a-woman takes on meaning within a process through which she attempts to subvert the social determinants that lead to the repetition of muliebrity.

Put another way, "femininity" would be that whereby subjectivity would detach itself from the social stereotype of housewife-bound-hand-and-foot-to-her-husband, as "masculinity" would refer to the path forged by an individual in refusing to be reduced to conventional male chauvinism (an assumed identity) (Dejours, 1988).

When, in Miss Mulvir's own words, it became possible to simultaneously acknowledge her wish for fulfilment in her profession as a technician *and* her aspirations to be a woman, she met somebody—and that encounter broke with the repetition of the affairs that she had had until then.

Whom did she meet? A PhD student in engineering, who came in to the factory to work on the same technology as she did. She taught him some tricks of the trade that she had discovered as she was doing her work. Then, one Saturday evening, he asked her out. A bolt from the blue! On their first date, they did not end up in bed together at once. So, what happened? He had a car, they went out for a drive, but they had an accident. The evening did not work out as planned. Earlier that day, the young man had had a celebration lunch with some friends, so was not hungry. He took Miss Mulvir back to his place and, by himself, prepared a pizza for her. It was a frozen one, so it was not all that great. But all the same . . .! He did the cooking himself, set the table, served the food to her and did not have anything to eat himself. They chatted together.

For the first time in her life, she felt true fondness stirring up inside her, which immediately exploded into feelings of love. In her session, she cried out: "That's it, I think I've met my Prince Charming!"

On their next date, she knew that she would not be able to have intercourse with him because she had been diagnosed with vaginal trichomoniasis. She was at his place, it was getting very late and she could not get back home. He told her to sleep in his bed, and he would sleep on the sofa. This really amazed her! She suggested that he sleep in the bed too, although she asked him not to touch her. He refused. She insisted. They had unprotected sex, although she said nothing to him about why she had been reticent.

In spite of these challenging psychological conditions, it was the first time in almost three years that she had had a successful sexual experience. With that young man, she was *both* a woman *and* acknowledged as such, valued as a person *and* respected. This experience, however, became possible only through a change in social context.

"Collective defence strategy" against suffering in the workplace and the risk of masculinisation

Afterwards, Miss Mulvir cannot stop bragging to her male friend about her sexual freedom. He is not shocked by this. She discovers that he has only limited experience with women and she becomes gripped by doubt. The entire session is given over to her bewilderment. What is now unsettling her is that this man is not chauvinistic, unlike every other man she has met so far. She no longer knows where she stands. Is she truly valued? Acknowledged? Loved? There is no question, in any case, of her being used as a more experienced teacher.

Her sexual dissatisfaction reappears, but in a very different way. Despite sexual intercourse on several occasions where she has appeared very enthusiastic and active, she is not satisfied. She cannot tolerate the uncertainty, the hesitation, and the ambivalence she is now subject to. She is incapable of waiting, nor is she capable of giving things time. She no longer talks about anything other than sexual techniques and no longer leaves any room for emotional issues: she is in headlong flight through her inability to tolerate anxiety.

I say to her:

You talk about your sex life with your boyfriend exactly like a guy talks about some girl. Today you have dished out all the details as if you had become a guy, as if now the only thing of any interest is to see how this guy's sexual technique measures up, and what's more, it's me you are telling all this to! It seems as though what you want to show me now are the notches on your bedpost, exactly like—not so long ago—the behaviour you were saying you hated in macho guys. You are no longer concerned about this boyfriend's feelings, you no longer acknowledge him, you no longer have any respect for him, and you speak in the same coarse terms as the guys you were criticising.

Taken aback, she keeps quiet for a fair while.

When she starts to speak again, she tells me about what had happened when she was at high school, at the start of her vocational diploma course.

She was the only girl in the class, and all the other students "were right on her case" from the start. She was made fun of all the time and upon any pretext, and was told that she would never pass the exams—she would never be able to keep up; she would never stick it out. This especially from her teachers, who could not stand her and heaped sarcasms on her constantly. While she was preparing for her technical *baccalauréat* exams, just before the final examination, her teachers had warned her that, at any rate, she could never succeed, regardless of her results. And yet her marks throughout the year had been good. She had reacted to this malice with a renewed burst of energy; it was the best way to prove them wrong. And she had gained her diploma.

> At the very beginning, there were two other girls. All the boys were between sixteen and eighteen years old, and all they talked about were dirty sex stories, especially in front of the girls. Those other two girls were immediately picked off because they refused to take part in that system.

One of the girls, who was "rather prissy and bad-tempered, she didn't last long. She dropped the course". As for the other, she was always the target of offensive remarks as she was chubby. It was from this moment on that Miss Mulvir had understood that it was not a question of being a kilo overweight; but if she wanted to get through this she would have to front up to the contempt, the insults, and the revulsion of the boys.

But she in particular had found a different strategy, a "trick of the trade", as it were. It took her three months to work it out. It involved adopting exactly the same language as the boys, speaking in a vulgar and coarse way about sex and women, and putting on a display of machismo—indeed, on that particular point, she put herself forward as even more of a male chauvinist than the boys themselves.

What we see here is a typical collective defence strategy constructed by men in order to ensure group cohesion between pupils and teachers, based on a socially-constructed virility that we often encounter in jobs that expose workers to dangers of one kind or another (building and civil engineering, nuclear production, fishermen, fighter pilots, etc.) (Dejours, 1988). Given that Miss Mulvir, who was sixteen at the time, did not want to abandon her studies in electronics—she really had a great passion for the subject—she would have to cope with a virile strategy, and do this in such a way as to make the boys acknowledge her as their equal; if she did not manage to do that, she would be subjected to all kinds of attack aimed at excluding her and making her capitulate, in the way that Cynthia Cockburn (1988) describes.

I did not attempt to conceal my interest in what the patient was telling me (she was saying that it was when she was sixteen that her problems began). She responded by recounting a critical anecdote that had just come back into her mind: "It was a kind of initiation ceremony", she said, "a rite of passage".

In her class, one of the students had mild learning difficulties; his grades were poor, he was not well-integrated and indeed he should not have been allowed to stay on in that class at all. But his father had come to the school in order to speak up for his son. The whole class was brought together for that purpose, and he explained to the students that his son had had a difficult birth, with forceps and such having to be used; as a result, his head and his face were left deformed, and so on. One day, that poor boy fell in love with one of the girls in the high school. He wanted others to pass along little notes to her because he did not dare give them to her directly—and it was Miss Mulvir who agreed to act as intermediary. In accomplishing her mission, she did everything she could to reassure the other girl and assure her that the boy was not at all dangerous. One day, the boy told his fellow students that he was going to kiss the girl and that as a result they would have children. They all burst out laughing, jeering at him, with sarcastic quips flying from all sides: "Bloody idiot! That's not how you get sprogs. You've got to get a hard on." He had no idea what that meant.

This was a propitious circumstance to exercise the power of domination by men over women: they forced Miss Mulvir to explain to the boy what it meant.

The group shut her up in the classroom with the boy, and waited behind the door. She realised that, if she was to have some chance of coming out on top of that situation, she would in fact have to tell him. She succeeded in explaining it to him. On leaving the room, the boy had to prove to the others that he had understood. So he said to them: "Yes, it's when your thingmy gets all stiff."

Various studies on the clinical aspects and psychopathology of work have demonstrated that there is a high psychological price to pay in adhering to collective defence strategies. In the majority of cases, that adherence—and it is required if one is to feel that one belongs to a working collectivity—necessitates not only passive consent but also some demonstration, whenever the circumstances demand it, of one's capacity to contribute in an enthusiastic and determined way to the functioning of the aforesaid virile strategy. Almost all collective defence strategies in the world of work have been devised by men; they are marked by a value system strongly connoted by the external signs of virility (Dejours, 1980). For women, therefore, the collective strategies devised by men constitute an obstacle to their advancement in their working careers, as the higher one gets up the ladder of qualifications, the more the career opportunities are collectively considered to be the exclusive preserve of men. This means that if women are to have any chance of encountering conditions conducive to the recognition of their professional qualities and self-fulfilment in their work, they often have to conform to virile behaviour or adopt a virile habitus. And since they are women, the ordeals, initiation rites, and other kinds of challenges are even more frequent and demanding than those that the men are put through.

Accordingly it is not unusual for the women who are the most successful in their integration, in order to be given higher responsibility and more interesting assignments, to feel obliged to adopt behaviours that are even more virile than those of their male colleagues. Many women fail in this struggle, internally torn apart between their sexual identity as women and their socially-determined identity. Many of those who refuse to capitulate have to "virilise" themselves—not only outwardly but also deep within themselves; in other words, they lose part of their femaleness.

The truth is indeed that, in the working world, it is a bitter struggle; competition is becoming increasingly formidable and nothing is handed to anyone on a plate. This means that, to last the course at work adopting a virile posture and habitus, one must, more often than not, commit to it completely. Displays of virility are only socially effective in the working world provided that they are not merely superficial and that they implicate one's entire personality. It quite often happens that, for these women, social and professional advancement bring in their wake problems in their relationships with men, the undermining of conjugal relationships, divorce or separation, and so on (Hirata & Kergoat, 1988).

This, then, is how I understand the development of the dynamics of Miss Mulvir's conflict. Initially, she wished to gain access to an interesting and skilled job, one that she would find fascinating, one that for her meant access to a social status, that of technician—this would be more promising than that of secretary-typist, and would open up real possibilities for developing sublimatory outlets. To have some chance of pursuing a career like this, she would first of all have to learn her trade. Given that this was a trade occupied almost exclusively by men, she was only able to remain in that field provided she agreed to bend to the collective defence strategies and the rites of initiation devised by those men; this was a *sine qua non* condition of her social integration. Learning virile behaviour brought her to the point of having to adopt a virile habitus (learning "by body" (Bourdieu, 1980)). To maintain this posture implied having to seek out virile models of identification in the service of the defensive processes (rather than by any process of idealisation). Her masculinisation (which would expand towards the male pole of sexuality) had by then indeed begun. A sexual identity crisis would ensue, leading to disorders in the function of her erotic body and to hesitation regarding her homo- or heterosexual orientation.

Running counter to this ("associative-dissociative" deconstruction (Laplanche, 1999)), we initially have her request for psychoanalysis, triggered by her sexual symptoms.

Through analysis, her recognition of the conjunction between her desire to gain access to social conditions conducive to sublimation and her desire to be a woman enabled the patient to re-establish a distinction between the two elements, of desire in the erotic field, and the expectation of recognition in the social domain (the encounter with the trainee engineer).

Finally, the analysis of her recourse to male-chauvinistic language when referencing a successful sexual encounter enabled her to recall the first stage when that masculinisation process was triggered, during her adolescence, in order to resist the pressures of social relationships marked by male domination of women. Thereafter, it became possible for her to envisage the accession to femininity in a reconstructed social world.

Centrality of work and sexuality theory: theoretical questions

Some months after this session, Miss Mulvir made the acquaintance of another boy, who was working as a technician in a small family business run by his father. What is more, this young man was studying for his technical diploma (BTS) in electromechanics. In their free time, they practice mechanics together, fixing technical problems, fixing up and repairing machines, even a car. Miss Mulvir has met her boyfriend's parents, who think very highly of her and have welcomed her warmly into the family. She knows now that she is in love, and believes that this boy is even more smitten with her. They will not move in together before he finishes his BTS. At the same time, she enrols in a new course of study at night school, at DUT level (university level technology studies).

At the workplace, she is now recognised for her excellent professional qualities and, in spite of a significant reduction in staff and the takeover of her company by a larger group, she manages to keep her job. Her sexual disorders have disappeared as well as her bouts of abdominal pain, and the patient terminates therapy after a period of three years.

We can therefore assume that the identification with her *father* worked, in this patient's case, in favour of an attempt to shape her personality as a sexualised *female* subject, not renouncing social recognition and the possibility of finding a suitable stage for her sublimatory outlets. Miss Mulvir's last remarks substantiate this: "I told Paul [her male friend] that I was perhaps still a little bit girly, but that maybe I also had sides and tastes that were more boyish." He replied: "Well as far as I'm concerned I've never met any girl as feminine as you", implying that Paul, for his part, is also able to escape, in some measure, the male-chauvinist stereotypes regarding the place and the role of women.

Of course the question arises of what would have become of this patient if she had not had three years of psychotherapy. The sexual difficulties she came up against seem to me to refer very precisely back to her adolescent problem complex between sexuality and society (Dejours, 1988).

It also seems to me that the outcome of her intrapsychic conflict was not a given. There were at least three possible routes or approaches.

The first would involve the repetition of the parental psychosexual problem complex, with the same impasses both in the sexual and the social register, the like of which seems to be the fate that had befallen Miss Mulvir's sister. The outcome would therefore have been a femininity that was isolated, even alienated, in *muliebrity*.

The second outcome would be in the appropriation of the social relationships of work contiguous with what had taken shape from the age of sixteen. The refusal to give up her social emancipation and self-fulfilment in the professional field could have concatenated successfully with a libidinal orientation veering towards *homosexuality*. The weight of the analytic listening could have been decisive in this sense, provided that it remained faithful to the classical interpretation of identificatory conflicts and—in contrast to the previous interpretation—it validated her horror of maternal identification. The outcome would have been a sexuality that was held captive by virility.

And finally, the third possible route would be that of the resolution of the conflict between sexual and social investments, not through the renunciation of one of the two terms in the name of the recognition of castration, but by the *combined success* in the two registers— sexual and non-sexual—that is to say, through a disengagement from the "defensive virility" without tipping over into muliebrity.

It should be noted that her indisputably neurotic character organisation makes it impossible to anticipate the direction the conflict will take at the end of adolescence.

The main difficulty of the analytical work lies in the analyst's listening, and the impact of this on interpretation and the development of transference.

Maintaining investments in the social field is insufficient if we do not manage to support these by working-through psychosexual conflict regarding the defensive origin of virile identification. The conflict above is not located between desire and guilt over gaining the father's love and coming up against rivalry with the mother. The negative oedipal dimension is certainly not absent. But this conflict of identification, inherited from infantile neurosis, has been largely worked through during the first phase of psychotherapy (two years), and came to an end with the patient's new-found independence, as she manages to separate herself from her parents and establish relationships with them that are divested of the heated component present at the start of therapy.

If the conflict had indeed been rigorously bound up with infantile neurosis, this resolution of it should, in one fell swoop, have cleared up the vaginismus and the dyspareunia (a sexual identity construct through identification with the parents, in diachrony). But the symptoms persisted. Analysis then refocused on the social component, that is to say, on the conflict arising from the sexual identity construct of *one sex by the other*, in synchrony. This second conflict continues to be mediated by relationships of work, conferring upon these relationships the quality of what conventionally goes by the term "centrality of work" in the scientific community of sociologists. The virile posture of Miss Mulvir is not a formation originating from desire but a defensive formation, intended to protect her psychically from the deleterious effects of social competition with men, which inevitably carries with it her allegiance to her sublimatory investments. The resolution of her identificatory conflict here entails the analysis of the defensive dimension of this orientation of her sexuality towards a virile position. Her sublimatory investments—as far as clinical analysis in the psychodynamics of work suggests in any case—possess their own rationality and do not always align comfortably with sexual orientations. Not least in women who face social relationships marked by the domination of men over women, save for the particular case of the nursing profession (Molinier, 1995). Adaptive participation in the defensive strategies constructed by men faced with the suffering engendered by their own relation to work, may function as an alienating entrapment to the point of negating, unexceptionally, female sexual identity. Any disentanglement from the defensive problem complex necessitates very specific analytic work that, when accomplished, leads to *bringing love-choice into line with sublimatory investments, and not the other way around,* as is generally thought. We must conclude that analysis of the requirements for the construction of sexual identity in the social sphere may take precedence over analysis of the construction of identity in the erotic sphere, in seeking to understand the signification of sexual symptoms.

* * *

The case of Miss Mulvir is not unique. On the contrary, standard psychoanalytic practice suggests that the problem of work plays in almost all cases an incomparable role in analytic treatment. Admittedly, the problem is visible more so in the treatment of women than men, on account of the asymmetry triggered, between men and women, by the social relationships of sex, and the sexual division of labour. But the problem is, in truth, also indeed present in men, albeit under a different guise. This may be demonstrated by the seriousness of psychosexual problems associated with the loss of employment and unemployment in men, for whom the loss of recognition and the conditions for self-fulfilment in the social and professional spheres gives rise to profound and sometimes tragic sexual identity disorders. Listening analytically to sexual conflicts engendered by the relation to work is a difficult thing to do. To avoid treating work as a reality that is merely external to the subject, and not to consider it as out of the reach of psychoanalytic investigation; to recognise its fundamental place at the very heart of psychic functioning, and the organisation and disorganisation of sexual identity, necessitates a keen awareness of the psychodynamics and the psychopathology of work. Indeed, analytic listening cannot rest upon natural aptitude alone, even if this is an irreplaceable dimension of it. *Analytic listening is also an acquired skill* that oscillates between elaborative work and the confluence of *concept* and *theory,* of interpretation and construction. If indeed, as Patrick Pharo (1996) shows, the paradigm for the apprehension of meaning entails passage through the concept, opening up the empathy of the interpretative arbiter, we need to grant some time to the study of the psychodynamics of work and the sociology of the social relationships of sex. "We find only what we seek and we seek only what we know", as the clinician's adage goes. Generally speaking, I am tempted to believe that there are certain difficulties to be found in listening and interpreting the *erotic and corporal* dimension in the patient's words (Dejours, 1993a). Likewise, at the other side of the clinical picture, to listen to what is being woven around the relation to *work*, namely, the non-sexual investments, and to grasp the ramifications of these investments, up to and including in the erotic sphere, demands of the analyst an ability to analyse and to interpret his or her own subjective relation to work; to start with the analysis of the impact of his professional practice as a psychoanalyst on his or her own erotic life (Dejours, 1993b).

References

Bourdieu, P. (1980). *Le sens pratique*. Paris: Minuit.

Cherniss, C. (1980). *Staff Burn Out: Job Stress with Human Services*. Beverly Hills, CA: Sage.

Cockburn, C. (1988). Machinery of dominance: women, men and technical know-how. *Les cahiers APRE-IRESCO-CNRS*, 7: 93–99.

Dejours, C. (1980). *Travail et usure mentale. Essai de psychopathologie du travail*. Paris: Le Centurion [fifth expanded edition, 2015].

Dejours, C. (1988). «Le masculin entre sexualité et société», *Adolescence*, 6: 89–116.

Dejours, C. (1993a). «Le corps dans l'interprétation». *Revue française de psychosomatique*, 2: 109–119.

Dejours, C. (1993b). «Pour une clinique de la médiation entre psychanalyse et politique: la psychodynamique du travail». *Revue TRANS*, 3: 131–156.

Freud, S. (1910c). *Leonardo da Vinci and a Memory of his Childhood. S.E.*, 11: 57–137. London: Hogarth.

Hirata, H., & Kergoat, D. (1988). *Rapports sociaux de sexe et psychopathologie du travail*. In: C. Dejours (Ed.), Plaisir et souffrance dans le travail (pp. 131–176). Paris: AOCIP.

Kergoat, D. (1982). *Les ouvrières*. Paris: Le Sycomore.

Kergoat, D. (1984). Plaidoyer pour une sociologie des rapports sociaux. In: M-A. Barrère-Maurrisson (Ed.), *Le sexe du travail* (pp. 207–220). Grenoble: Presses Universitaires de Grenoble.

Laplanche, J. (1999). La psychanalyse comme anti-herméneutique. In: *Entre séduction et inspiration: l'homme* (pp. 243–262). Paris: PUF.

Molinier, P. (1995). *Psychodynamique du travail et identité sexuelle*. Psychology thesis. Paris: CNAM.

Pharo, P. (1996). *L'injustice et le mal*. Paris: L'Harmattan.

CHAPTER FIVE

Psychological harassment at work: the subjugation of the body

Marie Grenier-Pezé

O n the outskirts of the big cities—my patch—the pathologies may seem caricaturesque: psychological harassment or bullying, musculo-skeletal disorders; these are the daily lot of the patients of the "Suffering and Work" surgery.

Work is emerging as a social fact that contributes to the construction or the deconstruction of physical and mental health, demanding the engagement of specialists to establish the semiology, the aetiology, and the therapeutics.

Work has been the subject of much specialised rhetoric. The legal practitioner speaks in terms of the labour contract, the company boss sets targets, the methodology department establishes the orders, the executive manages the teams, and the physiologist speaks in terms of biomechanics. The subject, in the field, pays no attention to physiology and sociology; he or she has only a fraction of the engineer's knowledge; he or she takes orders. But, in the end, the subject finds him or herself alone facing real life. That is, facing what makes itself known through resistance to control and to all of the assembled discourse.

It is for this reason that, as a psychoanalyst, to limit my therapeutic listening to the erotic body of patients through their childhood history—all the time while work (its regulation, its organisation, its ergonomic conceptualisation, its cost, its organic and psychic effects) is breaking by force into the clinical material—is a stance which is unrealistic and untenable.

In parallel to the clinical wealth of research into mental health at work, the notion of harassment (Hirigoyen, 1998) threatens to occupy the entire conceptual horizon such that the complaints of employees tend to be expressed almost uniquely by this formulation. The proliferation of associations, of specialist legal consultants and the enactment of a law (Loi No. 2002–73), have accentuated this movement. It is rare in the history of clinical practice that patients should arrive en masse to the consulting room having themselves made their own diagnosis, on the strength of a nosography thus promoted by the social discourse.

The notion of harassment incurs the "aggressor–victim" dyad and could, by referring only to psychological causality, unite a vast community of denial around the underlying reasons for the aggravation of suffering at work; the plea of the victims denouncing the violations of their dignity and calling for compensation contribute to the "psychologisation" of the debate. But what compensation can be expected for lost employment or for an attack on mental and/or physical health? What possible compensation can be given when the "aggressor–victim" pair proves to be more complex than anticipated in its construction, or when the account of the harassed party brings to light his or her participation (at best passive) in the harassment of another before their own occurred? What possible compensation when the accused torturer proves him or herself to be caught up in a web of pressures where they themselves must also fight to defend their health? What possible compensation when an entire working collective rounds on one of its members to save itself from collapse?

Incidentally, the legal definition, both in the Social Modernisation Act[1] as well as in penal law, has done away with intentionality in its definition of harassment, which nonetheless encompasses repeated acts *the purpose or effect of which* is to degrade the physical and mental health, to infringe upon the rights, dignity, and/or professional prospects of an employee.

Gestures of work and identity dynamics revisited

In return for the contribution we make to the organisation of work, we expect some compensation. Not simply a salary but also some recognition. The psychodynamics of work underscores the significance of this area of clinical analysis. The recognition of the quality of work carried out is the response to the subjective anticipations and expectations of which we are the bearers. When obtained, the doubts, difficulties, and the fatigue vanish before the feeling of having contributed to the collective *oeuvre* and achieving validation for the position we have managed to build among our peers.

Although foreign to the theoretical corpus of psychoanalysis, the notion of recognition runs parallel to the Freudian conception of sublimation as a socially valued activity, as an instinct (drive)-related process, described as, "[a] certain kind of modification of the aim and change of the object, in which our social valuation is taken into account . . ." (Freud, 1933[1932]). In the social field, work thus benefits from the extraordinary potency generated by the mobilisation of unconscious psychic processes.

Clearly, when the choice of profession is consistent with the needs of the subject, and when its modalities of practice permit the free play of mental and bodily functioning, work occupies a central role in psychosomatic equilibrium. The work situation acts upon the bodily economy on several levels. If the task carries with it a symbolic content, if the work, despite real-life pressures and the pressures of the organisation, allows for an inventive bodily exercise, it becomes a source of pleasure and of sublimation. Body and psychism work in unison towards mutually-rewarding production. The gestures of the work practice or trade cannot thus be reduced to efficient and operational biomechanical patterns. They are "acts of expression of the psychic and social posture which the subject expresses to others" (Dejours et al., 1994). They participate in the construction of identity.

This component originates from the family in the construction of identity first and foremost, given that gestures are transmitted in childhood by copying loved and admired adults. The child adopts the gestures, the stance or attitude, the "flicks of the wrist" of the adults out of *identificatory loyalty,* by mobilising early and solid defence mechanisms that will anchor the gesture in bodily expression.

Another gestural root is social identity, since the gesture is a socio-cultural construct. In the west, carrying children or heavy loads is done with the arms bent, locking the shoulder girdle, while in Africa the same tasks are carried out using the head and the back, involving different muscular masses and energy expenditure. More specifically, through apprenticeships, the gestures of the trade come to form close ties between the activity of the body and belonging within a professional community.

The last root is sexual identity. Given that gestures have a familial and social history, they also have a sex. Sexual identity and gender identity must by necessity be translated to attitudes, to specific postures. The maternal injunctions directed at the little girl are generally along the lines of: keep your knees closed, do not sit with your legs apart, do not stick out your chest; the opposite for the little boy. *Nurture inscribed in the musculature of specific sexualised postures.* A woman does not move like a man, does not work like a man, does not have the same jobs as a man, for that matter.

The modelling of a body will thus be done over years, reflecting sexual identity, existential choices, the muscular drooping of defeats and failures, the tissue memory of powerful events, the imprints of work.

Let us remember, to have an effect on the gesture is thus to have an effect on the identity.

In certain professions, the gesture may be rich in meaning and may mobilise the body in the service of this meaning. The actor performs his role, the musician performs his score, and the worker performs his prescribed task. Certain postures and attitudes of body confer dramaturgical value upon work and permit the flow of excitation; others are executed in "mental silence", by repressing any psychic activity, resulting in formidable energetic stasis. The worker may be subject to a work organisation that determines the content and the procedures of the task, fixes even the modalities of the relations between subjects by assigning to each his or her position and role in relation to the other workers. Sometimes, cognitive function is restricted to some, while corporal function assigned to others. In such an organisation, the individual is considered to be an instrument and used as a driving force.

> The body engaged in work is a tool-body whose performances are related to weight, to size, to corpulence, to musculature or to age; that is to say it is a body reduced to its physical and physiological characteristics ... The second body engaged in work is an uncertain body whose state of health, rhythms, limitations, variability, weaknesses, fatigue, disabilities and illnesses are united with affective states: pain, suffering, pleasure, excitation, emotion, feeling, desire, and eroticism. The organisation of work opposes this second body in vigorous repu-

diation. It gives value to the disciplinisation of bodies, their "biological uptime". The body is only accepted as a reservoir of strength, of power. The body in the organisation of work is a vehicle, not a starting point. (Dejours, 2000)

The formidable effectiveness of psychological harassment becomes clear after this long detour via the mental challenges of the work situation. To tamper with the gestures of the working practice ineluctably entails a coercion of the body. If the gestures of the working practice are a fundamental source of stabilisation of the psychosomatic economy, to render their performance aleatory, paradoxical, irrelevant, day after day, has traumatic results for the psyche. In the process of harassment, the repetition—conscious or unconscious of criticisms, goading, being placed in positions of blame or paradoxical prescriptive rules, quickly leads to impasse in the work of mental elaboration and takes on a certain power of effraction of the psychism. Furthermore, the impossibility of resignation, under threat of losing one's social rights, acts as a barrier to escape. The subordination adapted to the legal definition of the work contract confines the employee in a quasi-experimental context of toxicity. This blockage in the flow of traumatic excitation propels the subject towards depressive collapse and the more-or-less long-term somatic route.

Detailed analysis of the state of impasse described by patients uncovers the *isolation of the subject*: de facto isolation in a post without a team and without a working collective, where cooperation is absent as is, a fortiori, solidarity.

The cooperation that bonds a working collective together around common values calls for sharing and exchange of the unique procedures for the execution of the task, on the basis of shared trust. This possibility for sharing and exchange of experience may be severely disrupted by a working organisation focused on performance, keenly tracking so-called "downtime"; or a working organisation that is overly constraining and desubjectifying.

The fear of losing one's job cancels out any collective engagement, giving rise to silence and the every-man-for-himself attitude, and leading to behaviours of dominance/submission. It is clear that the manipulation of threat and blackmail, as well as harassment, are now well-established management methods to force error thus enabling dismissal for misconduct, or to undermine and drive to resignation.

In the psychodynamics of work, certainly, particular attention is paid to individual defence mechanisms, but equally to collective defence strategies. The latter, intended to combat suffering at work, are specific to each place of work; produced, stabilised, and maintained collectively. It principally consists in combating the fear engendered by the occupation by setting a collective denial of perception against it. In the construction of this denial, it appears that social virility plays a preponderant role. The exaltation of the virile does not only offer narcissistic compensation, at times it becomes a true defensive ideology that, shared by all members of a working collective, prohibits the expression of fear and in a wider sense of suffering or pain in the workplace. A leader, a true one, in order to succeed must manage to be blind to fear and suffering, his own as well as that of others. Cynicism becomes tantamount to strength of character. Tolerance of the suffering inflicted upon others is elevated to a positive value. Social power is measured by the ability to exert so-called necessary force over others, permitting the use of deleterious practices as a method of management used to obtain the emotional surrender of all. The making of a bully is therefore based upon the psychic and bodily internalisation of systematised techniques, by which they gain access to the world of work and come to terms with the principles of belonging to the dominant group, giving prominence to toughness, discipline, and bodily hardship.

Psychological harassment or the disciplinisation of bodies

Two women[2], a month apart, came to be sat in the same consulting room chair, sent by their occupational physician. They work at the same firm. One is a call centre operator, the other a manager. Their paths crossed violently on a call centre floor and each has wreaked havoc in the other's life. The organisation of work of one ran headlong into the management style of the other.

From the same armchair, each woman would reveal the impact of the psychosomatic and relational challenges of the work situation, each would say that a person goes to work with his or her own idiosyncrasies and history. That on this basis, occupation is thus always linked to identity.

Solange

Solange, aged fifty-two, is referred by her occupational physician. Married with two children, she started work when she was seventeen years old, as a secretary in a large company. Her husband was diagnosed with cancer and is currently on early retirement.

What is striking in Solange's file relating her personal circumstances are the constant changes she has been subjected to: 1970, redeployment; 1971, office transfer; 1976, redeployment; 1977, office relocation; 1978, office relocation; 1980, change in position; 1982, office relocation.

Her role was changed in 1996 to place her in a customer care department further away from home, which considerably complicated a life already loaded down by her role as primary care-giver to her partner.

She would remain for one year, without an office or a cloakroom on a floor of twenty people. The fashion is for open-plan office space, doing away with the individual office and even in open-plan spaces, eliminating assigned places. Less costly from a financial point of view it seems, but so psychically costly. How does one reposition themselves every day, or reinstall their working tools, in an anonymous, desubjectified space, with no photos, no personal effects, when, to accomplish the work undoubtedly requires subjectivity?

In the presence of this impersonal atmosphere with no solidarity, faced with the difficulty of access to information about her work, Solange manages alone and tells herself, "become hardened to it, don't respond to the negative atmosphere and lack of solidarity". She has a good attending physician who provides support in the form of treatments to improve her sleeping. She finds a way to unwind by playing petanque, taken up first of all as a shared activity with her sick husband, but now played for pleasure.

From 1996, the patient describes repeated changes in ways of working, a regrouping of teams that in fact leads to staff cutbacks; changes in procedure multiply and intensify: from annual changes, they become quarterly, monthly, and at times weekly. The significant amount of information to memorise regarding new services, the latest promotions, and new procedures generate considerable mental stress. The rapid appearance and disappearance of procedures forces staff to keep pace without the support of internalised knowledge. Solange also says that telephone etiquette standards have recently been imposed. She must answer using set formulae, with a certain tone of voice and forced inflections that are supposed to recreate the effect of an effortless strategic salesperson. The constraint of this working organisation is therefore at once bodily, emotional, and ethical, and compels workers to assume a protective shell that runs counter to spontaneous behaviour.

Solange therefore presents with the cognitive disorders commonplace among these types of "hot-desking" jobs: loss of memory, difficulties concentrating.

Initially, she had been appointed a "sponsor" to teach her the work who, she says, "did not give me any information for fear of losing his professional advantage over me, in a climate of outrageous rivalry". The same sponsors were rechristened "super-coaches". The climate and the pace of work intensify. The patient is at her post with a headset, so close to the employee next to her that she has to speak up so she can be heard, which, in turn, ramps up the sound level of the entire floor.

A panel with a red light is placed before her and, while she is attending to one customer, it signals to her that another customer is waiting. The super-coach walks behind the operators to get them to accelerate the rate of response, often at the expense of the complexity of individual situations. The double bind or paradoxical injunction is the overriding situation: attend to the customer on the line and ensure their satisfaction while also attending to the customer on hold. It is the super-coach who decides upon the moment when their physiological needs can be met. Any personalisation of the immediate environment, on display in other companies (photos of children, flowers, personal items, etc.) here is impossible. It is merely a question of having a workstation.

The constant surveillance by the super-coaches, the systematically being set up to fail concomitant with the intensification of the workload, the persecutory climate leading to frequent procedural changes, these become powerful levers of trauma that are akin to organisational harassment.

Overwork, cognitive coercion, absence of solidarity, and the desubjectification of her role would lead in Solange to the onset of decompensation with gynaecological symptoms. After many months of metrorrhagia, she underwent an enlarged hysterectomy in April 2001.

She advises her line managers of her leave and hears someone ask if it is a tumour. She is on leave for three months and states that she returned to work in good health.

Upon her return, as she is keen to settle back to her desk, she comes up against Mrs T, the new site manager. Mrs T informs Solange that, following a new floor reorganisation, she no longer has a desk. Solange is surprised that upon return from sick leave she no longer has a place and asks if she can at least retrieve her personal professional documents and her private effects. She hears Mrs T reply:

> I emptied everything out, as it was all trivial stuff! As for what was in the personal drawer, I threw it all in the bin.
>
> Even my pencils, my coffee cup?
>
> Yes!

Solange experiences a state of inexplicable social alienation. She no longer has a desk, she has been stripped of her personal things; this is the staging of her disappearance. She takes her place at an adjacent desk, but not before it is made clear to her that she will have to clear out of it again the next day, when its occupant returns. She picks up a procedural update at her provisional desk, as she says, "to get back in the swing of things" when she suddenly experiences roaring in her ears, and painful intracranial pressure, symptomatic of a major hypertensive spike. She collapses. The SAMU doctor, called in emergency, would diagnose high blood pressure at a reading of over twenty-two. The patient came very close to a having a stroke at her place of work.

Solange, whose case is managed by our multidisciplinary network, would have her rise in blood pressure reclassified as a work accident and was to benefit from extended sick leave, to avoid her having to take early retirement.

Mrs T

Mrs T comes to the surgery one month later. She saw Solange collapse onto the floor and, in the bustle of the emergency first aid administered by the ambulance team, was present for the "techie stuff" on her staff member before she was taken to hospital. The scene appears to have taken on a traumatic value through the danger of death of which she was the bearer. Since then, Mrs T has suffered anxiety attacks on a daily basis; she sleeps poorly, and constantly second-guesses herself. She is referred to me by the same occupational physician.

Mrs T recounts her career as did Solange. She graduated from the *l'école polytechnique féminine* (a prestigious graduate school of engineering). Over the course of her career, she has held successive positions of increasing complexity.

Since 1990, the threats of dismissal have become more frequent, and the organisation of work has taken a tougher line. From "we work for the motherland", we have moved to "we're going to work Japanese-style". Her working hours are increasing, and she travels around a lot. Now she is alone on contracts formerly negotiated with a work partner. Soon she will have to manage two contracts at once. She is never given the choice of contract. Whatever the men pass up falls to her. She should make do.

The only woman in this group of men, she hears from the executives around her: "You must have screwed the boss to move up so fast!"

The more her teams grow in size, the more she is called upon to assert herself, to exude an air of authority. "In the company, they consider stress to be a stimulant. So each executive is strongly advised to induce stress in order to achieve the best results." Her direct boss initiated her into managerial practices: "They'll give you someone and you are going to practice on them. You have the protection of management." Asserting oneself over somebody involves "tightening the screws" on someone lower down in the pecking order by setting them unachievable targets, with few resources and limited time, telling them that it is a challenge. It also means putting the pressure on as soon as people return from holidays. To assert her authority over others necessitates this type of strong-arm relationship, whereas her concept of authority as a woman comes "by relating", explains the patient, "by cooperation, by taking the other person and their professional strengths into consideration".

The new organisation of work seems to have radically altered relationships in the teams and toughened the defence systems that are established to "stay in control". Men certainly encounter the same difficulties as Mrs T in terms of time constraints and working without adequate resources. However, they seem to support these paradoxes by adhesion to a defensive ideology of business based on manly cynicism.

Furthermore, a technique for questioning employees is introduced as a specific management method. Carried out in pairs, it complies with the methods of unsettling used in police questioning: a raised and threatening verbal tone, bursts of questioning without giving the opportunity to reply, a systematic climate of accusation, false offers of a way out, extended duration of the interview, the door left open to the rest of the team. The aim is to end up with the emotional capitulation of the employee and of all those who have listened in. The authorised use of aggression is empowering to men and unites the working collective.

For Mrs T, the challenges become complicated. She must align herself with the ambient aggression all the time while holding on to her female know-how. Difficult mediations are entrusted to her as she is able to bring to bear her relational qualities of pre-emption, mediation, and empathy. Her director asks her to handle the foreign male clients, pointing out to her sarcastically that she was chosen to put her in a tight spot with these men. In fact, these clients all say that they are honoured to work with a Western woman.

Mrs T's solitude becomes overwhelming. She says nothing of her difficulties to her husband or family. Her salary is needed to absorb their debts and to pay for childcare. At the office, none of this must filter through. She cries in the toilets when she can no longer take it. She *wants* to work, to move up, to take on higher duties. She weighs no more than forty-five kilos. Unknown to her, the wearing down of her mental and physical state has increased. In any case, tiredness is unacceptable at work. To verbalise it openly involves making up one's mind, making a choice: to give up either work or children.

They no longer let her know about meetings. Unlike the other executives, she no longer has a designated computer, she works at whoever's workstation is available. She is made invisible, excluded by an underground boycott that "goes without saying". The only woman in a group of men, she is unable to bring her femaleness to the table. She no longer wears anything but trousers, she removes her jewellery, and her hairstyle becomes neutral. "I could no longer bear the salacious glances at my legs, my hair, my femininity! Delete, delete, delete . . . I erased all trace".

The team members, however, still come to her whenever a problematic issue arises. Mrs T must therefore psychically manage this contradiction: to somehow tolerate the close-up vagina shots on her colleagues' screen savers *and* remain their sympathetic mediator.

In parallel to this, company regulations stipulate that no discriminatory practices are permitted with regard to employees, be that on the grounds of race, religion, political opinion, or gender, and that there must be a commitment to treat them with dignity.

Hypervigilance and over-investment in the quality of her work topple Mrs T over into a stance of defensive activism. She no longer takes time for lunch, returning from work later and later in the evenings to finish up her work. Every weekend, she is bedridden with headaches or stomach pains. She no longer has the time or the strength to look after her children. The fear is now unrelenting. By day, as if on a loop, she plays back the scenes of sexist criticisms; by night she is plagued by intrusive nightmares that wake her up, bathed in sweat. Soon after, she would no longer be able to get to sleep at all. Now we are at the heart of the specificity of the clinical presentation related to psychological harassment that, depending on the school, goes by the name traumatic neurosis or post-traumatic stress disorder (PTSD), the semiology of which has been well documented.

Amenorrhea takes place. The only woman in a male collective, Mrs T has desexualised herself. We see how the organisation of work, through what it demands of the adaptive defences, can impact upon the subject's mental organisation up to and including its erotic structure. Her decompensated episode would not last long, recalls Mrs T. "I had no choice, I got used to it." To have any chance of finding conditions conducive to the recognition of her professional qualities and to self-fulfilment in her work, Mrs T decides to manage with the erotic economy of her male colleagues. She eventually becomes hardened to it. "I put my suffering to one side, and that of others too. I implemented the management they asked me to implement. And I followed it to the letter."

Mrs T tells me, sobbing, that she assumed the warrior guise; that she even ended up contributing quasi-enthusiastically to the functioning of the virile strategy. She quickly progressed, occupying increasingly important positions up to management of the centre where Solange worked. At the call centre, her role was to test the commitment of her troops. She had her eye on everyone and on all places. Solange's files, pencils, and coffee cup were, quite frankly, of little concern to her.

Solange, at risk of dying right before her, came to annihilate the defensive social construct. Her mental suffering loomed large once again, this time more pressing, requiring psychotherapeutic support with the aim of a renegotiation of her chosen career path and social status.

Conclusion

Some years ago it was declared to be endangered, yet work is still here, bringing us face to face with the resistance of the real, with the social sphere and with that part of ourselves that we attempt to gain recognition for. Between the walls of the "Suffering and Work" surgery, the encounter between subject and the organisation of work is not merely a perception. The relations of work described possess a rationale, specific modes of functioning, and a harshness that the notion of psychological harassment scarcely goes far enough to convey. This is a rationale that demands total commitment, at times involving giving up everything else. This "everything else" may also be bringing to completion the construction of the erotic body. The work of psychic bisexualisation, the encounter with the other may be placed in an impasse, a cul-de-sac, in favour of a socially-constructed surface sexual identity, one that is never definitively acquired since it is tacked on as a veneer from the exterior instead of from internal identifications (Pezé, 2002). Here, the conscious system being assembled is constructed at the expense of the preconscious system in a closed loop of determinism often leaving little space for the vicissitudes of the psyche.

Save for staring death in the face.

Notes

1. Article L 122-49 of the Labour Code (the Social Modernisation Act as amended by Act No. 2003-6 of 3 January 2003)

    No employee should be subject to repeated acts of psychological harassment the purpose or effect of which is the deterioration of working conditions which may infringe his or her rights and human dignity, may have an adverse effect upon his or her physical or mental health or may compromise his or her professional prospects.

Art. L 222-33 of the Penal Code:

Any person harassing another through repeated acts the purpose or effect of which is the deterioration of working conditions which may infringe his or her rights and human dignity, may have an adverse effect upon his or her physical or mental health or may compromise his or her professional prospects, shall be liable to one year of imprisonment and a €15,000 fine.

2.   This clinical case has been published in: M. Pezé (2008). *Ils ne mouraient pas tous mais tous étaient frappés*. [*They didn't all die but all were stricken.*] *Journal de la consultation «Souffrance et Travail» 1997–2008*, [Surgery journal "Suffering and Work"]. France: Pearson Education.

References

Dejours, C. (2000). «Différence anatomique et reconnaissance du réel dans le travail». In: P. Molinier & M. Grenier-Pezé (Eds.), *Les cahiers du genre* [special edition]: *Variations sur le corps, 29*: 101–126. Paris: L'Harmattan.

Dejours, C., Dessors, D., & Molinier, P. (1994). «Comprendre la résistance au changement». *Documents pour le médecin du travail, 58*: 112–117. INRS.

Freud, S. (1933[1932]). *New Introductory Lectures on Psycho-analysis.* Anxiety and Instinctual Life. *S.E., 22*: 97. London: Hogarth.

Hirigoyen, M.-F. (1998). *Le harcèlement moral*. Paris: Syros.

Loi No. 2002–73 (2002). De Modernisation Social. *Journal Officiel de la Republique Française*, 18 January 2002, p. 1008.

Pezé, M. (2002). *Le deuxième corps*. Paris: La Dispute.

Pezé, M. (2008). «Ils ne mouraient pas tous mais tous étaient frappés». Surgery journal: «*Souffrance et Travail» 1997–2008*. France: Pearson Education.

CHAPTER SIX

New forms of servitude and suicide

Christophe Dejours

S uicide at places of work was something that did take place in the past, but these acts belonged exclusively to the world of agriculture and farming, where home and workplace were one and the same. It is only in recent years, post 1995 it seems, that the first suicides at places of work occurred in the industrial sector, the tertiary sector, and the service sector. It is impossible to give a quantitative assessment of these deaths, the reason being that, to date, the statistical surveys on suicide have systematically ignored work-related psychopathology. The only quantitative investigation we know of is the result of the Basse-Normandie occupational health inspectorate. In 2004, Maryvonne Gournay, Françoise Lanièce, and Isabelle Kryvenac conducted a study alongside occupational physicians. In five years, forty-three deaths and sixteen people left with severe disabilities as a result of their suicide attempts were identified (Calvados, Orne, and Manche); giving a total of 59 out of the 107 reported cases of suicide and attempted suicide. This is, on average, twelve cases per year. This would mean that, scaled up to the level of a national survey, we should expect to find between 300 and 400 cases per year!

The fact is that we know very little about the circumstances of these tragedies. Surveys are exceedingly difficult because, past the moment of intense emotion immediately following the event, everyone becomes reluctant to speak out. It is as if a conspiracy of silence had descended upon the working community, from management and colleagues alike, direct superiors as well as trade unions. Most of the investigations begun by our facility at the request of the CHSCTs (committees for health, safety, and working conditions) have been cut short because the early volunteers subsequently withdraw. A handful of investigations have been completed (Flottes & Robert, 2002; Molinier et al., 1998, 1999), however negotiations on the type and duration of investigation generally result in a study that does little to shed light on the suicide itself. The compromise reached in setting the parameters of study consists in requesting an investigation into the relation between organisation of work and health. This blanket approach to the object of investigation deviates considerably from the specific clinical study of suicide, strictly speaking.

One of the reasons is that to gain access to the aetiology of a workplace suicide, as with any psychopathological state, we must also go some way into what was the private life of the deceased. To do this we must then go through close friends and family. Nonetheless, insofar as this is a suicide at the workplace, we must also collect data on work-related interpersonal and social relationships. It is not a stretch to imagine that information pertaining to the private life of the deceased, collected from those around him or her, raises thorny ethical issues.

It seems to me that, to have any chance of reconstructing the aetiology of a workplace suicide requires a priori a theory of the suicide on the one hand, and a theory of the relationship between work and outside-work on the other. Suicide is always a challenge to any nosologic classification. But in the case of workplace suicide, more often than not we are dealing with an acute episode in the advancement of depression. A thorough dissection of the psychodynamics of suicide in this context would, if we could implement it here, demonstrate that it progresses from self-hatred taken to the point of death.

In fact, when we do take a closer look, in every workplace suicide a psychopathological decompensation has taken place. And if we do get to know in detail the circumstances of the passing to the act (*passage à l'acte*), as a rule we discover, upstream of it, a very personal psychopathological configuration. This is usually enough for commentators, as it is incidentally for a number of specialists, to conclude that suicide is a matter of psychic causality where work at best plays a contingent role.

But the suicides that we are examining here were committed at the very places of work themselves. This is not merely a trivial detail. For suicide, as all human behaviour, is directed at the other. The technician who hanged himself at his plant workshop, the engineer who threw himself out of his office window, the supervisor who shot herself in the head in the hospital department where she worked, or the Volkswagen employee who killed himself at his plant in front of his colleagues: they are ostensibly sending a message. A message that is sometimes explicit when it appears in a letter left, by design, by the deceased.

Workplace suicide was something unheard of until recently. What then is the meaning of this recently emerged new dramatic expression? Did work thus never play a part in suicide in former times? This is hardly likely, albeit the hypothesis cannot be ruled out without solid reasoning. Then again—inasmuch as we cannot, in response to them, speak in terms of "epidemic" or "contagion phenomenon" as has often been the case with hysterical symptoms—it is likely that suicides at workplaces translate, here and there, to the emergence of a type of suffering at work that is entirely new.

Through their death, these unfortunate few are now summoning society as a whole to address this new type of suffering that it is generating. From the clinician's point of view, as it is of course for any sentient being, suicide is without doubt the most radical indictment of the connection to the other that we can imagine. These suicides surely point to a dismantling of social bonds at work. Even if these suicides were few and far between, by the very fact of their existence they would still signal a deleterious development affecting all who work and not just those who have died (Dejours & Bègue, 2009).

Daring to go one step further, if such suicide occurs, it surely speaks of the atrocious psychological solitude in which the victim found him or herself. This psychological solitude is first and foremost an affective solitude, and this I stress, as these suicides take place within a community of work that, in all likelihood, is a community in name alone. It is more likely that this is a grouping of people for the purposes of the work of production, but this grouping has no affective point of contact, or certainly it no longer has one. Affective solitude in the middle of the crowd; this is most likely the first meaning to be deciphered in a workplace suicide. And by the same token it points to another direction. If the person who committed suicide was effectively alone, in the middle of the multitude of others, what of the nature and the quality of the connections between these other men and women who formed the working multitude?

The answer is hardly ambiguous and/or hardly gives rise to ambiguity. For, contrary to what one might expect, there are numerous cases where employees who were in no way placed apart from the collective take their own lives. Some of them are regarded as people who are indeed extraordinarily well adapted to their work and to their professional environment. Today one can thus be perfectly well adapted, integrated, and efficient in one's work and yet be in affective solitude which becomes unbearable.

It is important to acknowledge that suicides at the workplace speak of a deep degradation of life in community and of solidarity that cannot be underestimated. In this alarming context, certain authors remain indifferent, behaving as if the appearance of these suicides in their hundreds in few years did not constitute an event.

The present contribution to the investigation of this enormous psychopathological issue will be modest. It is based on the study of one case. It is not much, but we indeed have to start somewhere, nonetheless in the hope that this precedent will support further clinical research. In this analysis I have endeavoured not to skim over, nor minimise, the shadowy areas and the potential conflicts of interpretation, as this clinical account is exceptionally complex. Analysis is based upon material collected after the tragedy. But the after-the-fact, the *après-coup*, does not constitute an insurmountable obstacle for the clinician. Quite the reverse is true. The same goes for the historian or for the judge. The after-the-fact, even after the death of the main actor, does not prevent us from getting close to the truth, even if there is a degree of conjecture in our analysis. Just one more difficulty in relation to the other disciplines further hampers the work: these are the ethical obligations that compel me not to report everything I learned about the case and that, in part, was information given in strictest confidence.

The history of the suicide

Mrs VB was a forty-three-year-old woman. She was an executive at a high-tech company. She was a trained mathematician with a Masters degree in computer science. She loved studying, devoured books, and went on numerous training courses. She joined a company where she was immediately valued, working in IT tools development. She then went on to work in a statistics department. Alongside her work, she completes a training course at the Institute of Business Administration, and then joins the human resources department of a multinational company where she, also bilingual, forges a brilliant career. On several occasions, she is contacted by head hunters for other, more attractive, jobs, but she turns them down as she does not wish to work away from her family (she is married with three children). At her company, her work is varied. She successively completes several important assignments that earn her warm congratulations. In 1997, she takes the helm of the company training department. Her salary ranges between €4,500 and €5,000 per month (in 2002).

And then, in 1999, she and her husband decide to adopt a child. The family burdens are heavy and she requests to work on a part-time basis (July 2000). They cannot refuse her, but a dim view is taken of this request. Eight months later, in February 2001, she reverts to working on a basis of eight per cent of full-time hours that she would maintain until September 2002. In the meantime, her immediate manager is sacked following a conflict of rivalry between him and one of his colleagues. It is his colleague who remains in the company and succeeds him in his position. Upon his arrival at the post, it seems as though he wanted to push out anyone who had been on close terms with his rival. Mrs VB was one of them. Others around Mrs VB were forced to leave or accept a transfer.

Starting in late 2001, Mrs VB is gradually relieved of her duties. She must now refer her work to the HR manager who is at a management level equal to her own. In the new organisational chart, she must refer her work to a team leader, who is at a management level far below her own. She is also then given an assignment far below her skills, one that is generally assigned to a secretary. She is the victim of multiple small acts of bullying: she is asked, as a matter of urgency, to draft a dossier. She works on it day and night and the dossier is then set aside without even being looked over. She is called to a meeting at a specific time, made to wait an hour, and then told that the meeting has been postponed. This happens on several occasions. In a few short months, she is demoted: her previous position is a direct report to the Resources Director, or two levels below the CEO; now she is under the supervision of her direct colleague, thus falling three levels below the CEO. She is demoted once again and placed under the supervision of a team leader, which makes her four levels below the CEO.

Seeing that she no longer has any future in this department, she looks for ways out: a training course at ESSEC business school, which some time earlier had been heartily recommended to her to be able to take on responsibilities higher again than those she had held at her highest level. She follows the course almost until its completion. But now having fallen into disfavour, two days before she is set to travel for the last module, when her tickets and hotel reservations had already been booked, she is refused permission to take the trip, which prevents her from gaining her diploma and ruins all the efforts she has made (September 2002).

She requests a transfer to another department. She is then made to take recruitment tests normally only for newcomers to the company and external candidates. In this environment, this particular treatment imposed upon her is conspicuously humiliating if not defamatory. And yet she submits to it without protest.

She does not fight back, she does not complain, but she does become depressed. To the point where, in 2002, she is forced to take sick leave, during which time she receives outpatient psychiatric treatment.

She goes back to work at the beginning of January 2003. Her boss advises her to request an extension of her leave as he has no work to assign to her. She returns two weeks later, whereupon she is once again given the junior secretarial assignment that she had already undertaken beforehand. With this assignment, it was made clear that she had served no purpose and that the company had done nothing about it. Eight days later (January 2003), she committed suicide by throwing herself off a bridge directly across from her company offices.

She left a letter requesting that the works council representative make it public after her death.

This is the letter:

> The reason I am committing suicide today is because, as I have often expressed and to several people who will be able to vouch for me on this, I cannot bear the idea of going back to my position under the conditions offered to me, that is, exactly the same ones that made me crack and that I have gone through since January 2002, the silent

treatment, lack of respect, (public) humiliation, psychological suffering and no professional recognition.

I am paying far too high a cost for my part-time position (which I took for various reasons but above all to look after children at Lenval), my sensitivity, my adhesion to my humanist values and to respect for others, whoever they are (even a Staff Rep, even a Works Council member who is against senior management), my refusal to be a "good soldier" (I am a pacifist), my refusal to be treated insensitively (and yes, I have feelings).

Sure I am lacking in professional ambition, the will to "climb the career ladder", I am not looking to be the boss, to take the place of the boss, I have other "things" in my life that balance out the investment I have in my work. But you all know how much my work means to me (I cut short my adoption leave), for a month I was chomping at the bit to get back to work. But through this work, particularly at HR, I longed to ease "human suffering" and not create it, I needed to be useful to the company and not work on projects that never end because of constantly changing decisions from the "bosses".

I am not going to go along with my bosses: the lack of professional intelligence: what does one judge on: on results and skills or on whims and misunderstandings?

To make me wait two weeks to give them time to "reorganise", two weeks before they offer (demand, actually, as I don't have a choice), exactly the same job as before, to rush through finishing the job descriptions, while they very well know that they will never be finished! They put me back in the same circumstances, still trying to catch me out, even though they made it very clear that they weren't "happy" with my results; "this is not what is expected of a manager".

1) They only have to give me what they expect of me and I'll do it.

2) I am not a manager: not in the duties I have been given, nor in the recognition of my value, nor in the position they've given me (see organisational chart!).

Do they want to set me up to fail? Or is it an unforgivable lack of intelligence at this level (of salary!!!)?

The lack of human intelligence: must we necessarily be "brutal" for the company to work better? To be respected or recognised in HR? Why this lack of respect? Why the need to humiliate? Why make me take tests after ten years at the company? To get to know my skills?!?!? And what has been done with those tests? (IE: "you never listen to anything, you just do exactly as you please"). While I don't know anyone more docile than me, "why didn't you take your RTTs (reduction in working hours) like everyone else?" Of course I took them, "you're too sensitive, that is not what is demanded of a manager". Luckily there are some sensitive managers out there!

We mustn't show emotion at work. I am not a machine and XXX when she cries is this not showing emotion?

Why are there never any apologies when our feelings have been hurt and the person who hurt us knows it?

Well I'm saying no, I'm not going back, some accept the humiliation, some are submissive, some run away to other departments, the atmosphere of the department is full of frustration (honestly who, in HR, isn't looking for a position somewhere else). As for me I'm quitting it all as I don't believe that things can possibly get better. I like my colleagues and my job far too much to accept these conditions.

I am sorry for doing this for my children, but I will not impose upon them a frustrated, humiliated mum.

It's no coincidence that I am doing this in front of Amadeus . . .

Collected elements on the personality of Mrs VB

From the elements gathered together from those around Mrs VB, it is clear that she was a brilliantly intelligent woman, considered by all to be above the norm. Indeed, she was thought of as highly gifted. This brilliance was backed up by extraordinary energy, and an extraordinary capacity for work. When she undertook a project, she would go at it full throttle. Each of her assignments is to this day a success. She fitted in remarkably well to her professional milieu, where she was thought of not only as a driving force, but also as a person you could place your trust in. Her reputation, for her colleagues as well as for her friends and relations, was that of an extremely sound and stable person, who was remarkably open and receptive, and generous to boot. People readily confided in her, coming to her for advice. Her attitude towards others went beyond the usual standards. The reason being that Mrs VB was firmly rooted in a Christian tradition of mutual aid and solidarity. In addition to her work, she tirelessly made visits to the sick in hospitals and cared for the well-being of detainees in prisons.

The family is also, for her, an essential organisational component of her life. Married to a man who shares her values and her commitments, she has three children, the eldest of whom is twenty-two years old, the second eldest twenty years old, and the third sixteen years old. All three are doing well and are successful in their studies. In 1999, she adopted a boy who was then nine and a half years old, and who is thirteen when Mrs VB takes her own life. I stress that she was very attached to all the members of her family. If there were problems, these were not related to conflicts with one or other person in the domestic sphere. And if there was conflict, it was only, resituated in the *après-coup*, a conflict with herself, reproaching herself for not managing to overcome her anxieties and thus inflicting the weight of her own suffering upon her loved ones.

Mrs VB was so firm in her commitments and true to her word that this could restrict her to a certain rigid inflexibility. As a result, she could dig her heels in and refuse to capitulate in adverse situations. Generally speaking, she would end up overcoming her difficulties. While some of her work colleagues, aware of the developing situation, advised her to throw in the towel and to leave, she on the other hand refused to do so. This was advice given on account of the flagrant injustice, and not by reason of any external signs of suffering that may have given cause for concern. For this reason, those close to her among her co-workers were stunned to learn of her suicide, as everyone had thought that Mrs VB was the epitome of psychological strength and stability. She did not want to admit early defeat because she did not want to let questionable practices develop as far as HR was concerned, for which she would have been a precedent, as it were, by resigning with her tail between her legs. And yet she had begun prospecting for other jobs and had incidentally been chosen for a high-powered position in another company. In the end, however, she had not accepted the offer; she had refused to give in to bullying and humiliation.

The elements I have reported here were gathered from her husband, her best friend, from people working at the same company. and from several doctors who knew and provided care for Mrs VB.

The company and management

This was a company for whom Mrs VB had worked for ten years and had known it since its beginnings when it was still the size of a small SME. Incidentally, she had contributed to its growth. Soon the company had reached much larger proportions, with international ramifications.

Around 1,200 employees worked there in 2003. Ninety-eight percent of the executives were graduates of the *Grandes Écoles of engineering and management.*

GM's management style is somewhat unusual. It comprises a former CGT trade unionist who certainly comes across as a "generation '68er". But he is also very authoritarian; he is always right. That said, this does not stop him from listening and taking notice of what filters back to him through the different channels, namely the social welfare department, the medical department, and the CHSCT (the occupational health and safety committee). Nevertheless, a few years ago, he engaged the services of a legal expert to HR management who is described as a caricature of authoritarianism and brutality directed against anyone who does not bow down before the company directives. And she in fact becomes the executive arm of general management. She was recruited after having completed the implementation of downsizing measures at a large-scale company operating in the same region.

The pace of work is maintained. They are to utilise just-in-time working processes and should integrate all improvisations resulting from market fluctuations. As such it is not uncommon that some employees work late into the evening and over the weekend. Wages are high enough and efforts are made to keep track of wage levels granted in the region so as not to fall below the others and to maintain the company's ability to attract and retain employees. It should be noted that the year before Mrs VB's suicide, the CHSCT succeeded in carrying out only one survey on stress in the workplace at the company and at other companies of the same type established in the region.

Next to this strong-arm management, the unions are very weak. Only a dozen or so employees are unionised.

In this company, there is no tradition of solidarity between staff. Recruitment is carried out all over the world. The working language is English. Among the employees, there are thirty-eight different nationalities. It seems that the employees recruited are a little "over-sized" in comparison to the actual responsibilities and assignments they are given in the company. After several years, on occasion five or more, some employees still do not speak a word of French. As a result, social integration into the city is poor and superficial. Incidentally, the company provides numerous services to its employees, such as the washing and laundering of household linen, leisure activities, and so on. This means that employees see a lot of each other outside of work. Consequently there is a degree of conviviality between them, the families included.

Strategic conviviality

But this conviviality merits closer examination, as it is rather complex. This is conviviality without solidarity. They often meet up outside of work but it seems that, at the end of the day, it is the same working relations that organise the outside-work activities. For example, each year management organises a party. Almost all the employees go. There is dinner and dancing. But it seems that people go because if they did not it might draw attention to them. And you do not want to be subject to any kind of scrutiny. This is doubtless also why unioni-sation is so low. It would appear that there is the presence of fear. Not so much fear of dismissal because, ultimately, there are very few, even if there are still some, as in the case of Mrs VB's boss. The fear seems more biased towards the challenges presented by career, by promo-tion, and by bonuses. Bonuses are significant, not in absolute terms but, all the same, enough for everyone to be careful not to compromise their chances of getting their hands on their due part. Mention must also be made of the annual appraisal interviews. Results are compared against goals, and new objectives are set. The allocation of bonuses seems to be done on a case-by-case basis, in an arbitrary manner. But these appraisal interviews have only limited impact in real terms. It is common knowledge, in the company, that the assessment records are only useful for when they decide they want to get rid of a colleague. Then they will demonstrate—with supporting evidence—that this person is too costly in comparison to what he or she brings in to the company.

The race to promotion and career advancement seems to be bound up with the aforementioned over-dimensioning in employee profiles in comparison with the positions. Given the burden of expatriation in France, these company employees are backed into a corner, as it were; the only way out for them being advancement in the company.

Social manoeuvring, therefore, entails maintaining good relationships with colleagues and managers. Promotion and career advancement are done on the basis of personality in the eyes of the managers. As such, it is vital to be well regarded, and the strategic rationale is that of maintaining a good "little black book" of contacts, being on good terms with well-positioned people; building one-to-one, convivial relationships, in short. Accordingly, conformism is very strictly adhered to.

What then is emerging is a new social world for the company employees, an executive world; a world made for executives, but also and above all a world made by executives. The conviviality that prevails between colleagues is not structured by solidarity. Quite the opposite, what structures this conviviality is "cronyism", which, behind the *bonhomie* of the relationships, conceals a world bound hand and foot to competition between peers, where the benchmark at work is continually set against how successfully one is able to conform to the prevailing culture. To characterise this particular social world, I shall suggest the term "strategic conviviality".

Six hundred people attend Mrs VB's funeral. She was very well-known and liked in the region, which explains the crowd. But of all those present, there is virtually no-one from the company. Reactions from company members, gathered in a non-systematic way, suggest two further explanations for this abstention: on the one hand, attending the funeral may have been harmful to one's image of conformity with the company; and on the other, Mrs VB's suicide prompted judgements of condemnation: you do not commit suicide when you have four children! We would need more complete information to gauge the defensive valence of this reaction. This interpretative hypothesis is difficult, if not impossible, to verify by reason of the extreme reticence of company employees in speaking about or commenting upon the event.

We must, however, dwell for a moment upon this world of strategic conviviality, as it is a new social configuration, one that might well be a specific product of the executive culture in multinational high-tech companies. In the region where Mrs VB's former company is situated, there are a great deal of similar companies. From the accounts of the occupational physicians who practice on inter-company duty and, consequently, are familiar with several of these companies, the clinical evidence suggests that there are indeed multiple psychopathological problems among these executives. The connection with work, the organisation of work, and above all with the new forms of management imported from the Anglo-Saxon world, would seem highly probable. To the point where several clinicians have felt the need to bring about—or to conduct themselves—investigations into the relationship between stress and the organisation of work.

When questioned, there is a very great contrast between what emerges from clinical scrutiny and what is alluded to by executives. A contrast to the point of dissonance. Most respondents interviewed report high levels of satisfaction in their work and in regard to their lifestyles. Strategic conviviality raises an interpretative issue in regard to the speech of these executives. Is conformism, the fear of drawing attention to oneself and compromising one's popularity, stymieing free speech? Is this an effective misrecognition of suffering because of the effectiveness of the defensive strategies, or because of support, in substance, for these values promoted by the company? This last version is not an improbability. The executives of these multinational companies go through a rigorous selection process. Do they adhere to the values of free enterprise, of individualism, to universal competition? It is feasible. If so, understandably they would experience some reluctance in revealing their suffering that could only come across as a sign of weakness, then functioning as a negative stigma in the struggle to remain universally competitive among executives of all levels. Each actor in the value-system of free competition would consider it perfectly normal and fair that a colleague who no longer seems up to meeting the company objectives should be dismissed. Not admitting one's own suffering to oneself is perhaps a *sine qua non* condition to maintain and safeguard one's position.

The fact remains that strategic conviviality functions, regarding our clinical concern to grasp the relationships between new forms of management and suffering, as a true conspiracy of silence that is merely perhaps the flip side of a rather widespread denial of the perception of reality. Strategic conviviality meshes work and outside-work entirely, by means of a material and moral dependence vis-à-vis the company, the purveyor of employment and a comfortable standard of living. In such a way, strategic conviviality might ultimately be the modern form of a "condition": the executive condition, now reframed as a new form of servitude in which the executive's entire life as well as those of his or her family are drawn into the neo-liberal company.

Here we are far from the condition of the worker dependent upon the paternalistic company, insofar as we are not dealing with people of modest social status, but people who consider themselves as integral contributors to the might of the company to which they pledge allegiance.

It is in light of this condition of servitude specific to the executive that we may now come back to the event triggering the process, the end result of which was the suicide of Mrs VB.

The trigger event and the issue of submission

The process in which Mrs VB was swept up clearly began when she requested part-time hours to be able to look after her adoptive child. That said, it almost certainly seems that this process became more acute in 2002 (January), after she turned down an important position, with promotion, in Spain. The company took a dim view of this decision by Mrs VB. Based on the hearsay of several people interviewed, it becomes clear that, for the company in question, to request part-time hours is a de facto indication that someone is no longer a team player. For the company, work must be the absolute priority concern of employees. To ask to go part-time is to indicate that something other than work counts as much as the company in the life of the employee. The company in fact demands docility, self-censorship, and silence on any non-work-related personal problem, and, above all, total submission.

By requesting part-time hours, Mrs VB triggered a process of negative criticism, loss of trust on the part of her managers, which would inevitably be followed by manoeuvrings to discredit and marginalise her. By requesting part-time hours, Mrs VB risked reprisals.

Did she know this? Was she being naive? This is highly unlikely given her clear-sightedness, her intelligence, her skilfulness, and her in-depth knowledge not only of this type of company that she knew inside-out, but also of the theoretical bases of these new forms of management. The troubling factor here comes from the fact that at no time were the reprisals administered to Mrs VB under the pretext that she had been professionally incompetent, that she had failed in her responsibilities, or that she had made mistakes. Here it must be stressed, and in my view this point is fundamental in regard to our current concern: work, and the quality of work, is totally *off the table* in the process triggered by the company. The only reason for the reprisals against Mrs VB is that she does not demonstrate sufficient submission. And this is precisely what will feature in the situation that drives her to suicide. It is indeed servitude that is at issue in this conflict, nothing else.

Mrs VB's wrongdoing was undoubtedly having sought to play her altruistic and compassionate values against those of the company. Her inflexibility over her social commitments perhaps explains that, despite the reprisals against her, she did not want to believe that they could, with the stroke of a pen, strike a line through all her service to the company and all the professional skills for which she had been widely acknowledged for years. Indeed, the process of psychological undermining to which she was subjected appears to have been rigorously executed. How?

Beginning with the tests that were touched upon earlier.

Over her professional career, Mrs VB had previously completed several training courses, including at the IAE (Institute of Business Administration) in which, incidentally, she finished top of the class. In 2002, even when she had fallen into disfavour, the manager acknowledged in writing, at each evaluation, Mrs VB's quality of work as: "exceeding target", "far exceeding target" (and once and once alone: "within target").

What are the tests? Personality and motivation tests:

> This is an in-depth testing developed by the SHL Group—Saville & Holdsworth Ltd—an international business consultancy headquartered in the UK. It aims to determine with precision the impact of various professional situations on the motivation of an individual, highlighting those having a considerable or significant impact, and those having low or no impact. It also clarifies the individual's personality, in particular his or her mode of relating (influence, affiliation, empathy), his or her mode of thinking (analysis, creativity, change, structure) but also, uncommonly insofar as it exceeds the professional

framework, it sheds light on his or her feelings and emotions. Finally, the test is concluded by an examination of intellectual ability. The test shows that Mrs VB scores 99% aptitude, i.e., placing her among the top 1% of most competent upper executives from around the world (norm SHL consultancy). (Extract from Mrs VB's administrative record)

In terms of her motivations, it is revealed in the test that only a few very clearly specified variables are capable of demotivating Mrs VB. The detailed analysis of the reprisals carried out against her shows that these entailed measures that played electively and exclusively upon situations identified by the test as demotivating for Mrs VB.

Note, however, that these reprisals were strictly symbolic. No physical violence was ever exercised against her. Her salary, which was comfortable, was never once called into question. However, it is evident that the destabilising conflict is symbolic in nature and is focused upon values, which is revealed in its fullest pathetic dimension in the letter Mrs VB left before killing herself.

Aetiology of the suicide

Mrs VB displayed a psychological vulnerability which must be taken into account in our analysis of her suicide. Mrs VB's altruism, the term by which I shall summarise her relation to her values; and her activism, by which I shall summarise the sthenic power of her various commitments, both in the professional sphere and in the city. Her altruism and her activism thus gave a dimension to her social and professional achievements which would be incomprehensible without that which must indeed be considered to be a certain rigid inflexibility. Her stringency in all things was first and foremost a demand, doubtless an excessive one, with regard to herself. And it is this relentless demand she places upon herself that arguably constituted her psychological flaw. In order to present the arguments for this diagnostic interpretation, one would need to here summon up information that I cannot produce, for reasons of professional secrecy.

If there were no ethical constraint, I could, by going into detail, show precisely what this psychopathological problem consisted of, which was indeed very serious. But this would not change what, in the aetiological analysis, originated from the practice of reprisals unleashed by the company. Why? Mrs VB, certainly, did not manage to put a stop to the manoeuvres to intimidate unleashed against her. She had a way out: to capitulate and leave, which is clearly the outcome that the company sought from her. Why did she refuse to save her skin and why did she persist in her fatal decision to not resign? Because she was entrenched in her obstinacy and because she suddenly proved herself to be intransigent in the extreme. Was it pathological, this rigid inflexibility? Without doubt. But to take this pathological moral inflexibility or intransigence for the *primum movens* of her suicide would be precipitous and would mean avoiding a problem that troubles us all. If Mrs VB committed suicide because she was the victim of her own moral and psychological rigidity, then we can think that the rest of us, who are not as rigid as her, would have fared better, enabling us to continue to believe that we are immune. This is a possibility, although, in place of Mrs VB, we would also have been expected to agree to concede to flagrant injustice and lose our jobs. And that is not all. In such a situation, one would have to be able to disinvest completely in something that has, year in year out, monopolised our existence and our energy; something that has also demanded of us a great deal of renunciation or even sacrifice; something that has also perhaps drawn on the best in us and is a source of some pride, and deservedly so.

To capitulate, to disinvest, would be to admit that all of this subjective involvement, by being callously repudiated by the company, has served for nothing; that it does not gives us any right to recognition, that all of the rewards we received previously were strictly cynical and instrumental. That is to say, that we have been deceived, and we are now being dragged through the mud. But that is not all; there is an even more bitter pill to come. We should have to admit that we were not only deceived by the company, but that we deceived ourselves. We tricked ourselves into believing in the company, in work, in the zeal, the usefulness of our efforts, renunciations, our suffering; we tricked ourselves into believing that at the other side of financial success there is emancipation. Admittedly, we had been hesitant to believe it and hesitant to embark upon the adventure. This perhaps makes the defeat even more cruel. Instead of recognition and emancipation, Mrs VB finds exactly the opposite: at the end of her contribution to the company's economic effort and on the other side of success, there is the relentless return of the *injunction to submission* that soon becomes an order to pack her bags.

Even without unusual moral rigidity, this capitulation is doubly painful, and indeed dangerous. To overcome the crisis, she has to review her entire life, to revise all of her judgements and beliefs, to overhaul from top to bottom her relationship with herself, with others and with society.

It would be futile trying to pretend otherwise. Faced with this ordeal, anyone who is sincerely invested in their work would be vulnerable. Not just Mrs VB. And each and every one of us gets their fingers burnt. Clinical data on dismissal is in this regard incontrovertible. The only ones who get off lightly are those who have never invested in work, or in the company, and those who, with some cynicism, have always kept an alternative solution up their sleeve and have stood ready to betray those who trusted them.

But that is not all. If we wanted to study Mrs VB's psychopathological fault in detail, then the relationship between fault and quality of work would take on quite another meaning than what this utter tragedy allows us to see.

The letter and the accusation

Indeed, each and every one of us, like Mrs VB, displays some vulnerability to mental illness. Every clinician since the nineteenth century, and the work of Philippe Pinel, Pierre Jean Georges Cabanis, and Antoine-Athanase Royer-Collard, have acknowledged as much.

But, of this vulnerability lurking at the bottom of each individual, psychodynamics offers a more in-depth study. Detailed analysis of the subjective relation to work shows us that no work of any quality is possible without the engagement of the entire subjectivity. To face "the real" of work, that is to say, that which makes itself known to the working subject through resistance to know-how, to technique, to knowledge, that is to say, to mastery, involves—for the subject who does not give up faced with adversity—mobilising an intelligence and an ingenuity that are demonstrably accompanied by a drastic overhauling of one's subjectivity and personality. To work is never solely to produce; it is in the same movement to transform oneself.

This self-transformation by the relation to the task presupposes that the subject who staunchly comes up against the real accepts being wholly occupied by his or her work. Up to and including in dreams.

This is why we all dream of our work from the moment we show stubbornness and obstinacy.

In certain cases, work may be a formidable test of one's self. But there are also times where, from this trial, the expanded self comes through. It is precisely for this reason, that is to say, because of this testing of the self that many of us throw ourselves into work with so much passion. Because in exchange for this suffering we can hope to transform ourselves, still further fulfil the potential of our intelligence and our subjectivity.

For this reason these *faults*, which risk one day engulfing us, are also precisely the strength of human involvement in work. And it is because of this vulnerability that we are at times capable of remarkable professional performance.

The psychological fault, the vulnerability, these cannot therefore be considered only as an obstacle to work. They are also what give intelligence its genius (sublimation). This was also the case for Mrs VB. Her principled intransigence was also what made her a particularly brilliant and highly-regarded professional. We might say that as long as this vulnerability is productive, no-one takes any notice. This vulnerability perhaps brings out the best, but it can also give rise to tragedy.

And the company is well able to use psychological weakness as a driver for work, as well as a switch for psychological undermining. At its discretion. This can be done simply by taking management decisions: reward first of all, reject or persecute later.

The company exploits our vulnerabilities and there is perhaps nothing reprehensible in this, since, in some cases, we can also reap the benefits. However, when the relation to work is undermined, as in this case, by questionable forms of management, there are serious risks to the mental and physical health of the person who is caught in the crossfire.

Undermining by management and withdrawal of solidarity

A progressive situation of psychological deterioration through a deliberate strategy by the upper tiers of management is not exceptional. If the case turns into a tragedy, it is also for some secondary and adjuvant reason, admittedly, however, one that is sufficiently significant all the same to merit the attention of the clinician concerned with the aetiological analysis.

Prevented by the process of reprisals from fulfilling her potential in the professional sphere, Mrs VB was seriously compromised in relation to the demands she placed upon herself. She gradually loses confidence in herself, and her self-worth is soon under threat of being shaken to the core. She then begins to blame herself for her powerlessness to overcome her crisis and is overwhelmed by feelings of shame and indignity.

This mental state gradually has ramifications for her family life. She fears that, through her psychological state, she will become toxic to her own children, so delegates more and more of the domestic and familial tasks to her husband. There is no need to go into detail on the impact of this situation upon their relationship as a couple, but under these conditions, ordinary life understandably becomes strained. This overwhelms Mrs VB all the more.

The idea of suicide, as a release, begins to form in her mind. In this complicated battle with herself, we must, it seems to me, accord a certain role to exhaustion. It is also because she feels her strength diminishing, her energy wavering, that Mrs VB fears breaking down. And she flees this nightmare by committing suicide.

If I have focused somewhat upon this tragedy's psychopathological aspect, it is to show the extent to which the aetiological analysis of suicide in the workplace is difficult. In light of these considerations on Mrs VB's psychopathological disturbances, one might be tempted to ascribe to them the determining role in her suicide. But the content of her letter and her suicide in such close proximity to the company force us to reconsider this point of view.

A progressive undermining such as that suffered by Mrs VB, generally speaking, does not go unnoticed by colleagues, and solidarity then functions, usually, as a true safety control against breakdown, even if the stated objective of solidarity is not the prevention of breakdown but the struggle against injustice.

Mrs VB was the victim of injustices. But solidarity did not come to her aide. It rather seems that the solidarity had little place in this new model of relation to work where, to a management demanding the submission of every company employee, the response is "strategic conviviality" forming a culture of solitude and of "everyone for themselves" in the middle of a crowd that is divested of any bonds of solidarity.

Mrs VB's suicide brings us directly to the heart of the new forms of servitude that go hand in hand with performance culture. We learn from this account that the pathologies of servitude, formerly reserved for the lower classes—from domestic staff to the jack-of-all-trades—these are now the concern of the executives, including the upper executives, of multinational companies. In fact, I fear that hidden in the shadow of these workplace suicides is the spectre of entirely new forms of servitude that are colonising the world of work and from which none of us can today consider ourselves to be safe.

Indeed, I would reiterate and emphasise this point, as it is this that is the most unusual element in terms of the clinical study of social relationships of work: despite all the manoeuvres used to undermine Mrs VB, her performance at work, until the very end, remained of the highest standards. The performance culture here negates itself through its own excess. If Mrs VB is undermined, it is not because she is no longer performing, it is not because she has become useless. It is because she is no longer submissive enough. Servitude to the point of submission as a crucial aspect of the organisation of work is more important than the work itself or profitability. Mrs VB's independent-mindedness is unacceptable and she must be made to yield at any cost. She did not just yield, she broke, and she killed herself. Mrs VB's suicide is, in no uncertain way, the result of new practices of domination. I am tempted to think—although this remains to be ascertained by the analysis of further cases—that this wave of suicides at the workplace, which is totally new, has many of the hallmarks of the radicalisation of methods of domination. These suicides reveal a turning-point in the relationship between servitude and domination in the company. This seemingly is the terrible sense that falteringly comes though this series of suicides. To me it seems that, through the victims' deaths this is the message that is crying out to be told.

References

Dejours, C., & Bègue, F. (2009). *Suicide et travail: que faire?* Paris: Presses Universitaires de France.

Flottes, A., & Robert, A. (2002). *Enquête de psychodynamique du travail à SERAA-EDF-RTE.* Confidential report.

Gournay, M., Lanièce, F., & Kryvenac, I. (2004). «Étude des suicides liés au travail en Basse-Normandie». *Travailler, 12*: 91–98.

Molinier, P., Scheller, L., & Rizet, C. (1998). *Enquête de psychodynamique du travail auprès des cadres infirmiers et des cadres supérieurs infirmiers de L'A.P.-H.P.*, *Convention*: A.P.-H.P./CNAM, Rapport Ronéo. Confidential report.

Molinier, P., Scheller, L., & Rizet, C. (1999). *Enquête de psychodynamique du travail auprès des adjoints cadres techniques et des ingénieurs subdivisionnaires de L'A.P.-H.P.*, *Convention*: A.P.-H.P./CNAM, Rapport Ronéo. Confidential report.

INDEX

This book examines the processes at issue in the onset of psychiatric disorders linked to stress in the workplace. Six clinical observations are presented: an acute psychosomatic decompensation (*status asthmaticus*); a delirious episode; a dementia-like confusional state; a sexuality disorder; two successive decompensations (one in a victim of workplace harassment and one in her aggressor); and a suicide.

Each is explored in detail, from aetiology to treatment, bringing into sharp relief the differences between conventional analysis and the interpretation of material in light of the reference to work. These studies have been written by psychoanalysts and may be used as a training resource for practitioners and students alike. For any professional or researcher involved in the world of work, these observations will offer a deeper understanding of this particular work-related mental pathology which characterises the development of our contemporary society.

'Sensitively focusing on clinical issues, this book offers a remarkable introduction to Dejours' essential contributions to the diagnostics and treatment of work-related pathologies and to the understanding of psychosomatics. Challenging the conventional division between mental illness and normality, it underlines the role of work in the psychodynamics of health as well as in the genesis of illnesses. Dejours' theory on the centrality of work has become a crucial reference on the necessity to develop clinical skills in listening to the subjective dimension of work in order to avoid mistakes in aetiological diagnosis and treatment approaches.'
—Hélène Tessier, Full professor, Faculty of Human Sciences and Philosophy,
  Saint Paul University, Ottawa

'Available in English at last, this collection is an excellent contribution to a field of increasing relevance, the relation of work to mental illness. While the chapters are focused on issues that arise in actual clinical practice, especially including the interrelation of work to gender and sexual identity, Dejours provides a strong theoretical argument for the crucial importance of the relation to work in mental health and its pivotal role in both the productive and the private spheres. A must-read book.'
—Teresa de Lauretis, Distinguished Professor Emerita of the History of Consciousness,
  University of California, Santa Cruz

CHRISTOPHE DEJOURS is a former hospital practitioner in psychiatry, a psychoanalyst, and Professor of Psychoanalysis, Health and Work at France's Conservatoire National des Arts et Métiers. He is also a member of the Association Psychanalytique de France and the Institut de Psychosomatique de Paris.

ISBN 978-1-7822018-0-9

KARNAC BOOKS
www.karnacbooks.com

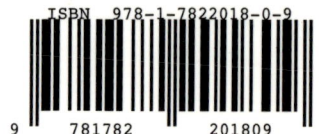

9 781782 201809